AM4L
A Mind for Life

The Awareness Journey
Written by
Mark Abraham

Copyright Notice

© Cover art, photography, illustrations and all text – Mark Abraham

ISBN-10: 0982982100
EAN 13: 9780982982105

Copyright © Mark Abraham 2010

The right of Mark Abraham to be identified as the owner and author of this work has been asserted by him in accordance with the Copyright, Designs and Patents Act 1988.

All worldwide rights reserved.

No part of this publication either from its paper or electronic origins may be reproduced in any material form (including photocopying or storing it in any medium by electronic means and whether or not transiently or incidentally to some other use of this publication) without the written permission of the copyright owner.

This book in both its paper and electronic form is sold subject to the condition that it shall not, by way of trade or otherwise, be lent, re-sold, hired out, or otherwise circulated without the author's prior consent. This includes but is not limited to any form of media, binding or cover other than that in which it is published and without a similar condition including this condition being imposed on the subsequent purchaser.

Dedication

This book is dedicated to several people who have had a profound impact on my life and who in turn have inspired me to write this book, which I hope will also have a meaning for others.

Special thanks to my grandfather Earnest Abraham, whom I have trusted as my role model both while living and after his passing! When I find trouble, I first look for advice in the example he set in his life!

To my family and friends around me, who have always offered encouragement and their support!

To the countless people I have interacted with in life, who have made every day interesting and every lesson worth learning!

Thanks goes to Maggie, Gina and my lovely wife for their work in editing and providing feedback that helped bring this book to its completion!

May you find these ideas worthwhile -- It is, after all, about the ideas and not the words!

Look within yourself, find a smile, and see if it fits for life!

Desolate Stand
Mark Abraham
Arches National Park 2007

One of the simplest ways to start seeing life differently is through photography. There are all the various angles and vantage points that allow each person's unique views of our world and all it encompasses. While photography is the visual art of capturing viewpoints, A Mind For Life is the mental framework that allows us to think differently.

Table of Contents

Forward 1
The Awareness Journey 5
AM4L 7
Expecting Too Much 11
Hindsight 19
Programs 23
The Fear Within 29
Struggles 33
A Cup Of Coffee 39
The Mind 45
Origins Of Programming 55
The Way We See Things 63
Life Cycles 71
A School Play 79
Truth And Integrity 85
How It's All About Me 95
The Death Spiral of Doom 105
Change 107
What IF 113
Parenting 119
The Difference You Make! 125
Mirror, Mirror 131

Pearls Of Wisdom	139
Complimentary Existence	147
Mind, Body And Soul	155
Needs, Needs, Needs	167
Dreams And Future	171
Living Our Lies	177
Decisions	199
Fitness	205
Owning Our Mistakes	211
Expectations	217
Sometimes There Are No Shortcuts	223
Care And Respect	229
Pain And Sorrow	235
Enemy Number One	239
Why Do We Hate So Much!	245
Diversity	249
All About Power	255
Celebrating Quietly	261
Emotional Efficiency	265
Expectations Be Darned!	273
Communicating	277
The Smile You Bring Others	283
Feeling The Love	293
Happiness Comes and Goes	305
My Life Now	311
What Now?	319
Closing	323
The Path	327
Life Meanings	339
Perfect Imperfection	349
About The Author	353

Forward

I tend to reflect deeply when I hear or think about someone proclaiming they don't want emotions to rule their lives. The single most impacting factor in our lives is our state of mind and the resulting emotions these states create.

Everything we do, the frame of mind we are in, and the subsequent thought processing these states create, govern our overall life experience.

Even when we are in the midst of the worst experience of our life, it is our state of mind that dictates whether we respond with courage and with the will to survive or we end up instead feeling terrorized, demoralized and defeated.

The same is true for the favorable times in our lives that often pass right by us without recognition. We get so preoccupied with the vision of obtainment and with the fulfillment of all our needs that we seemingly forget all about what we already have acquired and can enjoy. There is a sick, self-defeating logic to this as we keep collecting and collecting and never really enjoy life. Often we fail to realize that life experience is one of the greatest assets we collect as we move through our lives.

A Mind for Life

Awareness and the notion of being more mindfully present in our day-to-day lives is much of what this book is about. How do we frame everyday life, and why do we find ourselves sometimes happy and sometimes sad?

The answers, in my opinion, are very surprising, though it is not my intent to tell you how to think or to live life. I hope to share ideas and concepts that will help generate more consciousness and insight on how happy your life can be if you find more awareness and overcome some of the programming that are typically instilled in us.

I want you to know that I am not a mental health specialist, nor do I have any degrees in human psychology or any other medical science. My thoughts and ideas come from my own self-exploration for the meaning of life. What you will find here is the condensed self-learning I took time to write down, swizzle around in my mind, and build upon over several years, which finally culminated into these words you are reading.

I also want you to know that I really struggled with myself when it came to deciding whether to actually start down the path of writing and sharing all this with you. I was compelled by forces beyond my own comprehension, and it is my sincere hope that those of you who endeavor to read and explore these words and thoughts will find personal meaning and value in this journey.

Self-exploration is an emotional slippery slope to traverse. It's rather difficult to reach inside ourselves, beyond our own self-image and biases, right down to our very core, to find and pull forth the truth. It's a little like the story of pulling the sword from the stone!

Forward

My disclaimer up front is that I am not responsible for how you make use of what I present here. You may find these ideas and concepts to be things you already know or have already been told in life. They will often make perfect sense. However, we do not typically think of them as all being linked together or useful as a mindset. I have attempted to do: bring them together to develop a different view and way of approaching life.

Personally, I would like to think of this book as a possible instrument of inception rather than a course of deception.

I won't be able to share everything here. There may need to be another book someday, or a revision to this one. I learn something new every day. I reserve the right to change my ideas and thoughts as I too continue my journey and grow, expanding my own thoughts and ideas. I believe often the problem with our lives is our inability to embrace change, to adapt and move forward with new insight and vision.

A question that has come up before whenever I have shared ideas is whether I truly believe in them… Yes, I believe in what I have written and I really do try to live this way -- If you could ask those that know me best, they'd definitely tell you that this is who I am. Smile! My life is not perfect -- far from it -- and I believe life would be boring if it were so. If you want to judge whether you should read this book based on my material status, you will only find a man who believes he is rich in experience and spirit.

I have sprinkled a few photos in here as well. They are my own work, as photography has something to do with how I learned to see life in a different way. You can see them in color on my website, listed in the back of the book. Not only do I believe you can see your life differently from a psychological perspective, but also that you can visually perceive our world differently. Open your eyes!

I'll caution you once again: self-awareness is not for the faint of heart. For many it is much easier to remain oblivious to the notion of awareness and continue bouncing around against the bumpers of life, like a cold steel ball in a pinball machine.

After a long walk on this path, symbolically speaking, there is a bright and vibrant rainbow that will hover above your conscious self and help provide enlightenment.

When you see some text in Italics in this book, it's because I want to call your attention to those words for deeper consideration.

Finally, you can choose to change things on your own and be the train conductor of your life, or you can let others choose for you and ride life's train as a passenger.

It's a new mindset! I call it A Mind For Life!

The Awareness Journey

The reality you believe exists is a carefully constructed illusion. Imagined or real, we each dangle from the puppet master's strings! Mostly, we are oblivious to the pulls and tugs of the strings that dictate our daily lives.

Sometimes, to understand the truth you must be told and believe the lie first. Whether we really believe the illusion is created by some puppet master, by our own selves, or simply non-existent, has no real bearing on the fact that our lives are not completely real. They are often derived by the superficial constructs that we are given upon our birth and then throughout our life experience.

The fact is, almost everything you think and almost every way you respond to life is based on programming that builds with each

A Mind for Life

day we live and experience life. It's virtually no different than the programming created for a video game or the storyline for a book or film.

Because our life is our reality, it's very difficult for us to see the strings that guide us. There are a few SCI-FI films that come to mind over the past few years that have questioned reality; some dealing with the programmer being the all-guiding master, and others dealing with dream states.

If instead of an alternate dimension or dream state, the environment you live in is in fact real and through increased awareness you had a choice to break free and author your own new string-free life, would you cut the strings? How would you choose?

Welcome to A Mind For Life, the awareness journey begins now!

AM4L

I wanted to take a few moments to explain how developing greater awareness and A Mind For Life works at a somewhat more scientific level. I will state again that I am not a psychologist, and that this is just my opinion and a loose representation of how gaining awareness can impact your thought process.

It's also okay to skip this chapter if you're really not interested in the theory behind how AM4L works. You can always refer back to it later, if you'd like. I'll be honest and warn you that this chapter is rather dry, and so my disclaimer here is to not let this section trip you up from moving ahead with the remainder of the book, which I am sure you'll find more interesting.

A Mind for Life

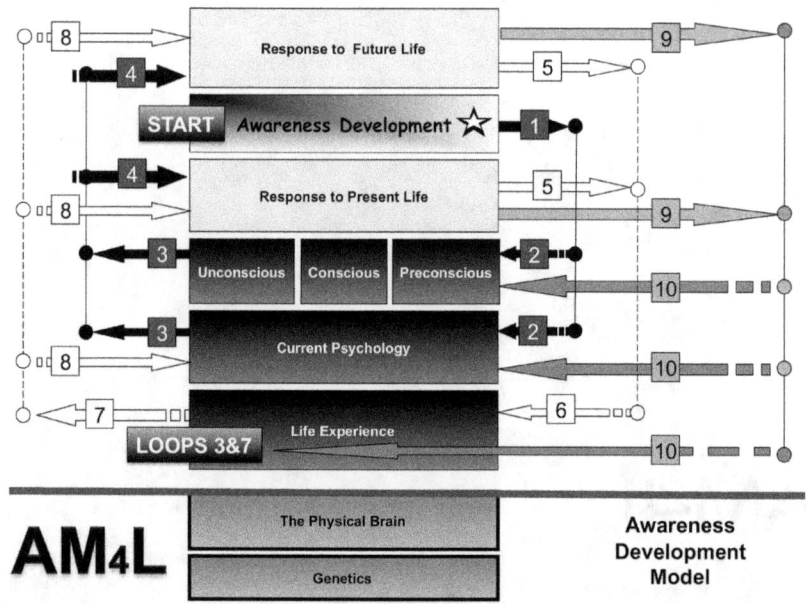

Above you can see what may appear to be a fairly complex diagram. The diagram is a process flow and depicts how my concept of reprogramming works.

Keeping this idea as simple as I can, we start with the development of greater awareness. Look for the START block above. The process actually never ends, as once we get to step 10 the process feeds back into steps 3 and 7, and repeats steps 4 through 10 again.

If we start from the bottom of the stack of blocks, we see genetics. Genetically we are predisposed to some certain psychology. Scientists are finding that genetics impact us less and less, though. Much of how we behave and react in life is the result of our life experiences.

Above genetics we have the physical brain. This is just the raw brain we are given at birth. There is not much we can do to alter our brain, although some medical conditions, chemical levels and our life habits do impact and can alter the physical brain. For now, let's say that it is mostly static in nature.

Above the physical brain we have our life experience or the sum of life as we have lived it up until here and now. This is the first layer that has significant impact on our current psychology and the three types of consciousness.

One could argue that the types of consciousness, (preconscious, unconscious and conscious) sit above the physical brain, and in a different conversation they would. In a model where we are explaining how awareness impacts our lives I prefer to layer them in the order I have presented.

I wanted to underline that I do believe we have a conscious as well as an unconscious. The preconscious is intriguing and I'll leave it up to you to go and Google it if it interests you.

Above life experience we have our current psychology and it is a result of our life experience. Our three types of consciousness, life experience and current psychology form our response to present life. You might say they form how we respond and behave in the here and now.

As we gain awareness, our consciousness types change, and in turn our response to life changes. This loops around to modify the way we respond and behave with regard to future events, and that future response will impact our life experience, as well as our consciousness and psychology.

For example, let's say I love mint chewing gum. If I gain the awareness that mint chewing gum causes me a headache and makes me irritable, I may then decide that mint chewing gum is bad for me. This simple process updates my current psychology and life experience; and as it grows, the awareness impacts my conscious mind, and eventually my unconscious. Both my current and future psychology will be impacted by the awareness that my experience with mint chewing gum is bad. Consequently I may turn down mint chewing gum when it's offered to me in the future.

This is an endless loop, and as our awareness increases we develop and we are able to make smarter decisions and respond to life differently.

A Mind For Life focuses on how to gain more awareness in life. While what I have just described may now seem obvious, there are actually many ways to gain a deeper awareness.

Additionally, we will discuss how we get programmed to respond the way we do in life, and I will use real-life instances of how emotions play out and impact our lives, as well as present some examples of alternative thinking that I will share on a more personal level.

Expecting Too Much

As I sat and drank my coffee this morning looking at the steam curl off the top of the cup and saunter away in spiraling waves I wondered for a moment where it was that we learned and came to expect so much from life? Was it taught to us or was it something inherent in us as humans? Did it come from TV, magazines and other media? Or was it maybe a mixture of all of it, systemic to the human condition?

I joked with my lovely stepdaughter last night and asked her to imagine how happy she would be in life if she could live without ever wanting anything. As you might imagine, she gave me a funny, uncomprehending look. Reflecting on it, I am certain she couldn't even imagine not wanting anything at all!

Seriously though, what if we could just live and feel free without the worry of what the next moment might bring? Most of us have been there at some point or another, in the moment, one with everything, and know it can feel like being enveloped by a warm, blissful, drifting stream of contentment. We feel seemingly aware of everything and yet not really thinking about anything at all.

Imagine for a moment, with all your walls of skepticism, doubts and training set aside, what life would feel like if we did not expect so much, and felt instead content and appreciative of all we already had!

It might be easier to visualize a person who lived in a horrible, depressed existence for the first 40 years of his or her life and was then thrust into a life of ease and happiness. Imagine how wonderful it might all seem and how grateful that person might feel.

Is it not crazy that sometimes, when this shift happens to people, some of them become bitter and unsettled instead? They get obsessed with how it should have happened sooner, and angry about how hard they had it before fortune finally found them. Some people seem predisposed to always believing life is never good enough and that they are being cheated. Why is it so difficult for them to just enjoy their newfound easy life?

Failed expectations create negative emotions. If you're a visual person, try to imagine life emotions on a graph for a moment. Normal life (not happy not sad) being a 5 on the following graph, we find that we live day to day and even moment to moment changing our emotional status.

When life fails to meet our expectations our emotions can dip below the neutral line. It can go below 5 and into the 4's, 3's, 2's, etc.

Expecting Too Much

When life exceeds our expectations, our emotions climb above the neutral line into the 6-10's.

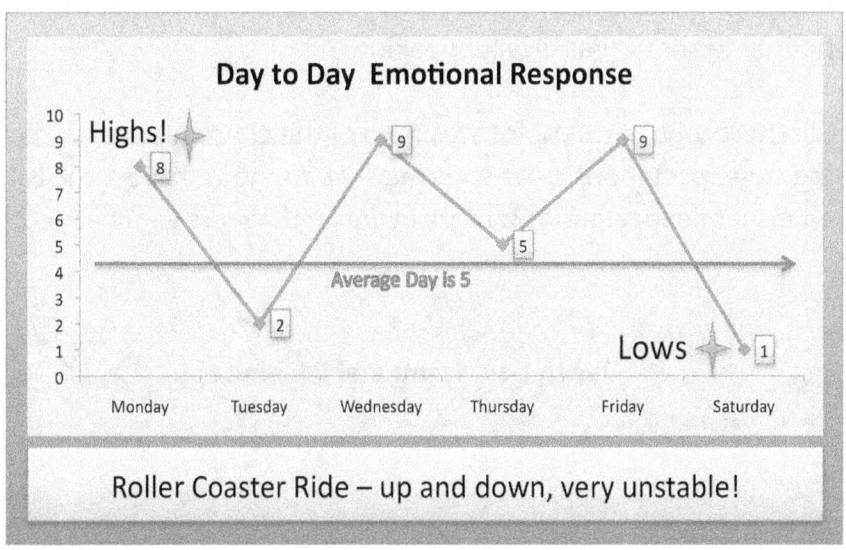

Roller Coaster Ride – up and down, very unstable!

It may seem redundant to talk about this fact, as its probably no major revelation to you that the more expectations you have the more often your expectations won't be met and your emotions will dip below the neutral line.

Something "silly" I say to people is that the more you want the less you'll have, and the more you expect the less you'll get. I'll elaborate more on this later!

If you have children or have a chance to be around them, you may sometimes feel like everything you give is never enough, and that they seem to never be thankful for all they get; and even if you do not have any children, you may nonetheless recall how many things you yourself wanted as a child, how you would tirelessly nag your mom and dad for something and cry when you did not get your way.

The irony is that we often act the same way as adults, and fail to realize that if we had fewer expectations our emotions would rise above the line more often. At a minimum, they would not dip below the line. In summary, we would spend more time in the neutral territory, graphically speaking.

For those who at this point are afraid of the consequences of having no expectations, bear with me -- Learning to have a realistic amount of expectations is more in line with where I am headed.

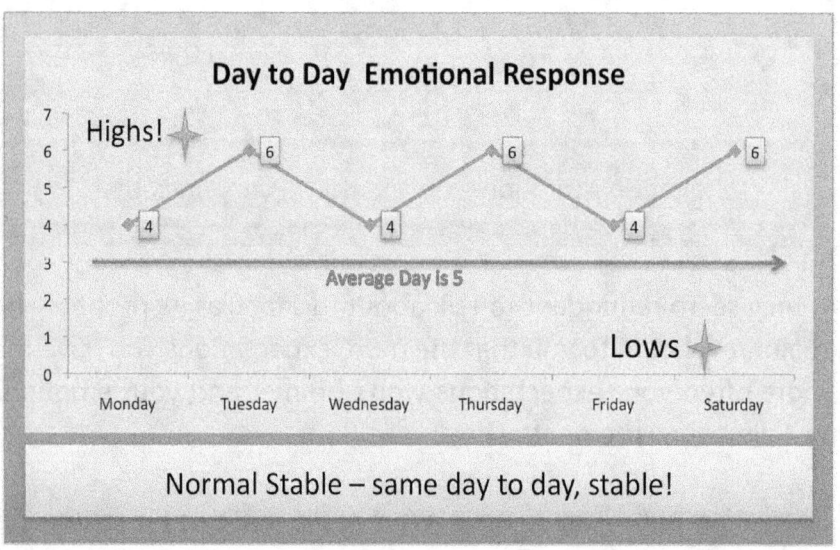

Having all kinds of expectations and constantly experiencing the failure of their realization blinds us to all the things we actually do have and keeps us from being grateful for them.

On the contrary, embracing what we already have and appreciating it increases our capacity for gratitude and alters our emotional response, thus causing our feelings to run above the neutral zone into greater overall happiness.

Expecting Too Much

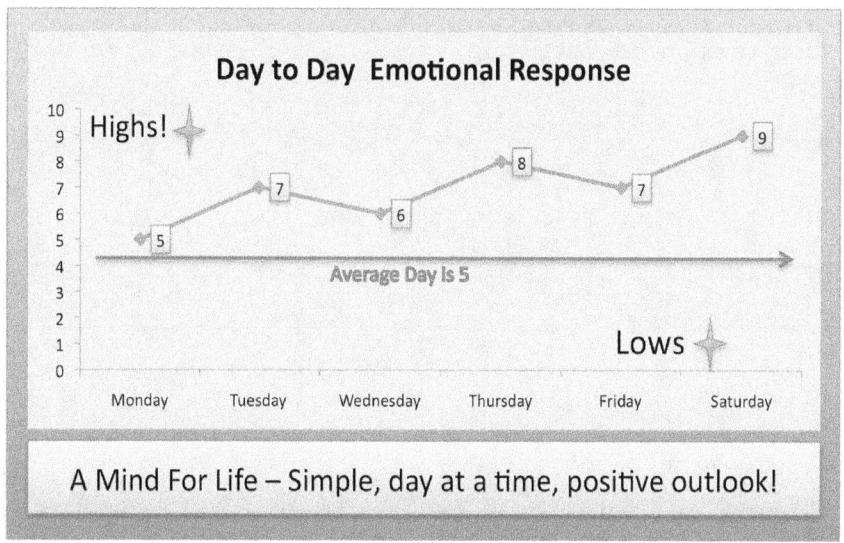

I call this process the science of reprogramming ourselves and much of this book is focused on learning how to see and feel differently about life.

It may seem stupid, and you might say, "Of course I'll have more if I want less!" And yet maybe right now you're feeling that if you have no expectations people will walk all over you.

But isn't it great when something exceeds our expectations? It feels really good, doesn't it! The very recognition of this fact can create happiness, because we feel like we are getting more out of life than we asked for. Truly, one of the greatest sources of unhappiness in our life is that we want and expect too much!

We will explore this simple, but essential truth much deeper as we move forward.

Blades
Mark Abraham
Olathe, Kansas 2004

Everything is so easy if we allow ourselves to see it that way! Before mankind became dominant over nature, squeezing it out of our daily life with our new man-made world, there was nature itself, and we lived from its bounty. Our need to create has changed the face of the world. We are addicted to the actuation of power we get from building our dreams, but will we later regret how overbearing we've become and dream for the peace and solitude that can be found in real nature?

Hindsight

It's crazy to think that despite being able to look back at our mistakes we continue to make them over and over again. We only seem to ever so slowly make tiny steps forward. Perhaps even more ironic is that if I offered you the ability to avoid many future mistakes and to greatly reduce this senseless pattern, you'd probably dismiss the idea and say, "No, thanks!"

Why do we continue to swim upstream and operate against our better judgment? If we learn by experience, why is it that we simply defy these lessons and repeatedly allow ourselves to fail over and over again? One might ask, exactly what kind of programming do we get when we begin life?

Understanding this programming is tricky business! One would think that if failure results in negative experiences we would be programmed to NOT fail. In reality, programming manifests itself in different ways, some as simple as learning not to touch fire because it burns us, and others more complex, such as the justification of overeating, though it leads to becoming unhealthy and fat. In the latter we override the future fat factor in our minds with the immediate pleasure derived from eating. We simply tell ourselves that it's just this once, or maybe that we'll take a walk later, in an effort to rationalize our choice.

Often we remedy becoming fat with diet and exercise. The problem though is that for many at some point, the labor of diet and exercise loses its appeal over the pleasure that the foods provide, and so they fall backwards again.

Why is it that the voice of consumption and desire is louder than the one of common sense and reason? The reasons are varied, but they all result in a cycle of failure. If we keep with this example of fat being a problem in our lives (this could also easily be smoking, gambling or a myriad of other self-destructive behaviors), then we begin to realize that avoiding the bad behaviors is far more complex than we imagined. Sometimes they exceed our inherent abilities to deal with them. To truly overcome these conditions, we need superior methods of dealing with them on a long-term basis that can last for a lifetime.

This is what real reprogramming is about. It takes work and a lot of thought to target the true root cause of the issue we are trying to resolve. Mere hindsight and bad experiences are not enough to overcome many of the challenges we face in life.

A Mind For Life looks at these behaviors, their potential sources, and the ways of overcoming one's current programming. It also allows us to focus on what troubles us the most, so that we can then selectively reprogram ourselves as we live out the remainder of our lives. It's there to help bring about balance, harmony and hopefully long-term happiness.

AM4L is not a guarantee though, and it's certainly not a shortcut to solving all your problems. It's a framework for an alternative thought process and behavior modification techniques that for many will result in profound life changes. Please keep in mind that I am not speaking in clinical terms when I use expressions such as "behavior modification."

Change takes a great deal of desire, courage and effort, and AM4L is no substitute for any of them -- You have to want to do the work, and then actually get it done. It will help make the journey easier, though, since it attempts to frame progress into smaller steps we can understand, map and follow. To use an analogy, if you set out to walk across a vast plain, with mountains immediately to your back and mountains in the distance those first steps are disparaging. The mountains ahead feel like they are never getting any closer. Nonetheless, if you walk forward, step by step, when you occasionally look back you will see the distance of the mountains behind you grow. Slowly, over time they become more and more distant, and you begin to feel like you're making progress.

The more small the steps you take, the more they add up, and eventually the mountains ahead draw closer, your strength and courage grow, and you begin to take pride in the space you have conquered and the goal ahead.

I have met many people who do not like to plan or think ahead too much. What they fail to realize is that they often do it without even noticing: they still look ahead to the day they get married and will have children, and they think about the steps in between, such as getting an education, finding a job, and then meeting the person of their dreams.

I encourage you not to focus on the full breadth of change that lay ahead between you and your goals and dreams for change, but rather consider the excitement of taking those first small steps and building upon them day by day to reach your destination. It's ok to envision greater simplicity and happiness as you get ready to move forward -- that is, ultimately, your long-term plan -- but don't worry about all the steps between here and there: we can take those one at a time.

You're on your way now!

Programs

Before we dig too far into all this, I thought it wise to ensure that everyone knows what a program is. Let's dissect it into layman's terms and connect it to its reference and usage throughout this book.

Literally speaking, a program is a set of instructions that are assembled to complete a task. Although usually associated with computers, programs are not limited to the world of technology. For example, someone might write a program or set of instructions to make coffee in the morning. It could look something like this:

Name: Morning Coffee
Author: Mark

START
Locate coffee maker

Clean coffee maker if in need of cleaning
Fill coffee maker with water
Insert coffee filter
Add 2 scoops of coffee
Close all lids
Ensure the pot is in place and ready to receive fresh coffee
Press brew on coffee maker
Wait for coffee to complete
Locate coffee cup while coffee is brewing
Clean cup if needed
When machine indicates coffee is ready, pour coffee into cup.
END

Every day at their jobs or in their daily life people follow instructions, which are very much a form of programming.

Programs are not always written instructions, though. You execute a program when you are slapped in the face. You will have a response, and it's interesting to see in how many different ways people react to it. Imagine an episode of Candid Camera or of a modern day reality show in which the theme for that week's show is slapping people. An actor walks up to people out of nowhere, looks at them and then slaps them across the face and just stands there, intensely looking into their eyes. Think of the many emotional responses he will evoke… Rage, shock, fear, the possibilities are almost countless, and every reaction is driven by the programming each person already has.

The point is, there are programs for literally everything we do in life, from blinking our eyes to drinking the coffee we just made to work, leisure, relationships and every last bit of our life.

Programs

Much of how we behave and live is programmed into our unconscious through our experiences. It also comes by way of the people whom we interact. Programming comes from everywhere and everyone!

This book discusses how the basis of our thoughts and emotions are merely programming, and it attempts to teach how we can reprogram ourselves, if we so choose.

I believe that much of the programming we have in us doesn't really fit us or even serve us well, and ultimately this faulty programming often accounts for a lot of the unhappiness and trouble we experience in life.

Have you ever read a set of instructions and found redundant or unnecessary steps? How about left over parts when you put something together! What if we could update the instructions and programs we follow in life? Get rid of the bad ones, improve the useful ones?

At this point, I wanted you to be aware that we are going to bounce around a little, but it will all build towards a higher understanding about self-awareness and hopefully of yourself and your consciousness. Resist the urge to skip ahead, and I believe you'll be rewarded!

Walk with me further, but don't look back yet, as we have only begun! Let's journey ahead towards those mountains we see in the distance.

Island in The Sky
Mark Abraham
Arches National park 2007

In the sky, there is an island! Across its reaches are mountains, and in between lie desert and craters. In our mind we can very quickly travel the distance with optimism. If we fly past the middle, we will miss all that is below and miss the contrast that makes both the middle and the distance so much more than what we have our sights fixed on. Much of the reward of the destination is the experience we gain and sights we see in the journey!

The Fear Within

Too often we find ourselves living in fear, though nobody wants to live this way. Unfortunately, all too often that's exactly what we do: we choose to live in fear.

You could almost think of it as a loop. In programming terms, a loop is a block of instructions that repeat themselves over and over again. Some loops are useful and some are extremely damaging and prevent other portions of the instructions from executing. When something scares us we react to protect ourselves. The actions spawned by this self-preservation mechanism often make us defensive and paranoid, which in turn scares us more.

Fear is a trap or loop we can easily get caught in. While ridiculous and obvious to state, we should strive to react more wisely and appropriately. However, that's not always easy when we are just following the instructions that are programmed into us. If we are not aware we are following a program, then we cannot look at it from outside our confines, see its future results, and make changes to improve it.

Computers have no consciousness, and so they merely execute the instructions we give them. All too often we live our lives the same way. Completely unaware of the unconscious programming we are executing, we do not questions its usefulness and performance. And this is, after all, why there has been such a strong push to implement an effective artificial intelligence in machines: to give them the ability to make decisions when things go wrong.

Imagine, if you will, a yogurt factory. It packages yogurt into containers and seals them for packing. If the machine that fills the cups of yogurt doesn't know when the machine feeding it the cups runs out of them, then yogurt will keep on getting squirted, though there may be no cups for it and a giant mess will follow shortly afterwards. It's all solved, though, if one machine becomes AWARE of the status of the other. Likewise, this is our aim: building awareness of the programming we live by and stopping the yogurt messes that occur in our own lives on a regular basis.

I think that too many people find themselves motivated by one fear or another in their lives and surroundings. Fear of losing their job, fear of sickness, fear of death… The list is seemingly never ending.

A few years ago I came to the realization, after having navigated through a major life change, that to stop living in fear we need to be prepared to face the consequences associated with change. *If we really want to make a change, escape the tight braces of fear, then sometimes we must be prepared to fail, to lose all that we have, and fall flat on our faces.*

I have told friends that you need to take control of your own life or someone else will take control of it for you! You'll then have to live with the decisions that are made for you, rather than using your abilities to make them for yourself.

Consider a couple who divorces. If it isn't a mutual decision, all too often one chooses to file for divorce and the other has no other choice but to deal with it, regardless of his or her desires. The impact from such a decision can be enormous and can result in profound changes, both good and bad, for all who are involved. For example, a woman who leaves an abusive husband has also to be prepared to take on many responsibilities she previously shared with her husband, which may include earning an income for the first time while the custody of their children may fall solely on her. Or she may acquire marital debt, have to find a full-time job, and provide care for her children while working all day and handling of all the family affairs.

Some may see leaving a marriage as an absolute necessity for their safety and future happiness, while others may view it as a gamble at best . This is why so many times people stay in bad marriages for so long: fear of change. Those changes can truly be severe, and bring both a mental and a physical impact.

Perspective plays a huge role in how we live our lives. The ability to see from different vantage points is a very powerful tool, and learning to see beyond the fear even more so!

Sometimes people live in fear of change to lesser, but just as damaging, degrees. Suppose they are in a career they hate, and you hear them saying, "Well, I am too old to try something new." I had a friend feel that way, but when she got divorced she suddenly found that everything in her life was subject to change and had to grab control.

A Mind for Life

If life can hand you such changes in your later years against your own will, then it simply means that you can also choose to make major changes of your own accord just as easily, and with equal or greater success.

It is therefore appropriate to directly confront the notion of fear of change -- and of fear in general. Embrace life's challenges, make your own decisions, and move forward. I understand it's easier said than done, but let's continue. It is my hope that you will be the driver of the changes in your life and not the passenger I have described before. I believe much of what I will share can help you accomplish this important task and realize as much change as you desire, and to do it with greater success.

The chapter on change can help you embrace and forge a new path for yourself, and there are other aids in this book to help along the way. The key is to take things one small step at a time!

The main idea is not to let the things you fear dictate your choices. Face the fears that have become the roadblocks in your life. Once you start down that road, you'll be surprised at how it is easier than you previously thought.

There is much more to this book, though, so, with hopefully a tiny bit of your interest peeked, let's dig in and talk about the way the mind works, how it impacts you, and how much of how you act and live was programmed into you -- and not of your own free will.

Do not fear if those mountains out in the distance appear at a greater distance than you have ever traveled… Together, we will make it there!

Struggles

Life is a struggle!

If we understand and embrace the fact that the sheer act of living is a struggle then we can begin to see life differently and understand the nature of true happiness.

Being the optimist I am, it's ironic that I would begin by saying that the most realistic way to approach happiness is to accept the fact that, overall, life is a struggle and full of difficulties. Many would even call it miserable! But how miserable you see your life can be a matter of how you interpret the events that occur in it.

A Mind For Life is different, and timeless in its approach to helping you navigate life. Unlike the majority of self-help books, which take the approach of showing you how to get everything you want, AM4L focuses on dealing with the reality that you're not likely to get everything you want. It's a lot about learning to want and need less and simplify your life. Given that I am writing this book in 2010 and you will be reading it in 2011 or later, learning to expect and live with less is a timely skill to obtain.

Being optimistically pessimistic is the key to finding the right balance and developing an outlook that is more compatible with happiness. It must surely sounds insane, but if you expect everything to be difficult, you'll find yourself almost always pleasantly surprised.

As a frame of mind I suggest that you go forth in life reaching for the stars; just don't have the expectation that you'll actually reach them. Again, you'll be surprised if you make it and will not be very disappointed if you don't.

For most, life seems miserable because we are brought into this world by exiting the warm, safe confines of the womb into something far less protecting, far less comfortable, and full of obstacles. Even food is no longer a given, as it is not readily available 24/7 at your demand. If you cry loud and long enough, you may get food. The air is cold, and there is no longer fluid to wrap and comfort you like soft pillows and blankets.

In a manner of speaking, we are still wild creatures of a sort, and if you have ever watched a documentary on insects and how they eat and are eaten, and witness the struggle and labor of an insect's life, with careful thought you could easily parallel their mode of existence with our own. No, I am not trying to insult you and infer we are all mere insects! Really, that's not the point.

Struggles

*Life is a struggle to survive and our **selfishness** is created upon birth and our emergence from the womb. **Selflessness** is seldom achieved and can take a lifetime to develop.*

At the moment of our birth true desire is born, and the beginning of needs, and therefore disappointments, becomes reality. I could go on with these analogies, but I know that you already get the point. Perhaps you might even be wondering how can we ever be happy.

When we cannot change the way things appear to us, a rock being a rock, a wall being a wall, seemingly like obstacles that hinder our journey, then we can either yield to our perception that they are impassable or choose to look at them differently.

Perhaps the rock is not an obstacle in our path, but a tool to help us accomplish something. I could literally give you hundreds of other ways to see the rock and yet, even as an obstacle, a rock can be viewed as a challenge, and then a lesson learned when it is passed. Learning to get past a rock is a skill that has to be developed, one that helps us navigate past future rocks with great agility and speed. You see? There are other ways to look at the obstacles in our lives!

It is my hope that with this book you'll feel comfortable about shedding some of the programs instilled into you. Programming tells us that every moment should be happy and full of joy, else you are not succeeding. I would have you understand that without the contrast coming from both positive and negative experiences you could not truly appreciate the good parts of life.

A Mind for Life

The next chapter contains what I call introspection. It means looking inside or from inside. These introspective musings can almost be considered timeouts, and in them I'll share a bit of myself and real-life examples of thinking within this framework. I trust they will add to the overall meaning of the book.

So, if you will, kick back, relax, and have a cup of coffee with me!

Sailing Sandhill
Mark Abraham
Platte River, Nebraska 2005

Letting go of one's problems and engaging in the chase of just seeing the sights our world offers can be exhilarating! Without the fear of being judged we can run and play like children.

A farmer's cornfield annoyance is another person's bird watching delight! It is how we see our world that determines whether its beauty and simplicity plays a role in our own personal life meaning.

A Cup Of Coffee

A story comes to mind that I'd like to share. Is a cup of coffee just a cup of coffee? Think about it a moment… Have you ever gone to a coffee shop and heard the person who just received their beverage complain that it was not made as they ordered it? Ever hear a man or woman hollering, "I said no whipped cream!" Oh, was that you that I heard having a cow? Smile!

But seriously, folks, where do we think we get the right to yell at another human being over a $4 coffee drink? Do we think so much of ourselves and so little of others?

I recall journeying to the Platte River one fall to see and photograph the sandhill cranes. This is one of the locations where their migratory path crosses, and they are noted for their unusual coloring. We drove up one afternoon for an appointment the next morning before sunrise to be escorted to a photo blind – sort of like a hunter's blind -- to catch the sleeping cranes awaking, and see them fly off for the day as the sun came up over the river.

We were directed to meet our guides at a gas station very early, around 3:30 AM if I recall correctly. They would take us quietly by van to the Bird Sanctuary and from there escort us by foot to the blind.

The morning of the appointment the weather was awful! Severe thunderstorms and drenching cold rain greeted us as we left our hotel room. We arrived at the pick-up point and were driven to the main building at the sanctuary where they announced that the event was basically canceled. However, they offered to take those of us who remained to the blind without guarantee of safety or success.

We took the offer and began walking to the blind in pouring rain, lightning and thunder all around us. A lightning bolt slammed the trees halfway there, and I remember my boot coming off in the mud, which was as gooey as quicksand! The light was blinding and the deafening thunder instantaneously causing us all to jump -- or at least shudder, as we were too mired in mud to actually jump. I remember thinking that lightning never strikes twice in the same place and having a mere second of comfort before another bolt touched down near the same spot, but this time a little closer. It was one of those moments you wonder about your level of intelligence and what in the world you were thinking when you agreed to go on the adventure.

Insane as it was, though, we made it to the blind. I shivered in the cold, and took my pictures, which were dismal, yet somehow mystifying. As we waited and watched the darkness slowly give way to a grey light, the cranes made their eerie sound, awoke, and then flew away.

When we returned to the main building, I was greeted with a warm steaming cup of coffee! It was just normal, common brewed stuff, nothing special on any other day, but absolutely divine on that morning as it warmed my cold hands and soothed my spirit.

It's amazing to reflect on how great life seems when you emerge from something perilous in nature. It's all in the mind! Shouldn't we feel grateful to have that cup of coffee that is going to help revive us and help us earn a day's pay? Where does the anger within originate when they put that cream on our latte though we said no whipped?

Do you still think a cup of coffee is just a cup of coffee?

Story aside, I am asking you to begin accepting the fact that it is all a struggle, understand how to see it all differently, shed your selfishness, and find the joy of thinking more about others than yourself! Shed the complexities, cast away those misplaced expectations that are seemingly all around you in your life, and embrace the simplicity of life itself.

Today's great struggles and challenges often become tomorrow's great stories and memories of triumph!

I will be upfront now and tell you there are no easy answers! Happiness takes a lot of work because we are programmed to see anything short of continuous gratification as a source of unhappiness and hardship, as exemplified by the screaming patron who's upset about the whipped cream on his latte, and is oblivious to the fact that he is so very fortunate to be able to even afford one or that the people that served it also make mistakes, have lives, struggles and are only human.

Ever wonder about the source of where the expectation that everyone else be flawless in their interaction with you comes from? Don't you expect others to be forgiving when you yourself make a mistake? It's ironic, isn't it?

I think we have gotten so bad that some of us cannot even enjoy the good times we do manage to have. Our comfort is short-lived as we quickly turn back to that mindset of wanting more and more. The disappointment that all that desire generates when it is not fulfilled returns us to feeling unhappy and unsatisfied.

Maybe you're wondering right now what's the origin of all this wanting. How did we become so bottomless? Continue journeying with me, maybe we can find some answers and some ways you can address these feelings within you.

Try to take time after each chapter and reflect upon the thoughts I share. Please understand that I do not demand anything of you in this book. Furthermore, keep in mind that, I am not prescribing advice and promising happiness in return. I am merely sharing thoughts that I I believe will change the very way you look at life. That in turn may lead you to feel happier overall.

The programming we have been given runs very deep, and overriding it can become a lifelong effort. What I can tell you is that the more you escape it, the more you realize that instinctually we were really meant to live and see things differently. It's truly amazing how different the reality and truth of life are from the manufactured fantasy that has been and will continue to be programmed into us.

Some of the programming helps the directionless follow a path that often feels hollow and pointless, yet it still provides a roadmap, and many find comfort in it, as they do not know of any other way to live. Most of us are born to follow rather than lead. I think that this is why at times we ask the big question: what is the meaning of life?

There is a true path for each of us! You can only understand this reality when you find that path and travel it. Many are amazed to discover that the path shown to us is not always easy to follow, and yet, despite the bumps, mountains, and holes that lie upon it, they almost always know it's the right one. There is excitement and wonder in imperfection!

The pain of the challenges on that road never seem to bother us as much as the lesser pains and problems we find on the artificial one. On our rightful path, we find ourselves with the biggest and most satisfying smile on our faces! Have you ever considered that spiritual happiness and material fulfillment are the results of completely different lifestyles? Have you ever felt it doesn't pay to be a good person because the notion of pay in your mind at the time was one material reward? What would spiritual richness be worth if you could buy it like any other material possession?

At this point you might be wondering what in the world I'm talking about, and thinking that I'm surely mad! Am I telling you that you are to follow a harder, more challenging path in life, that you should be more selfless, see obstacles as no big deal, and through all this, that you'll find greater happiness?

And my answer would be, yes and no, so if you read on, I will bring far greater clarity to these ideas and ultimately logic to what seems insane.

The Mind

I believe that whether we like it or not, in large part, we are not self-aware or mindful of the fact that we are the sum of our life experiences.

To a degree we live an illusion of life rather than a real life. Am I suggesting that your life is a lie? I do not know, or am I? Seriously, though, your life is indeed a series of lies, at least in part, and it can be proven.

You are exactly where you are at this point in time and the sum of your life experiences has you here reading these pages. Be it a hard life, a good life, a rich life or a poor one, you have arrived here and now. How you think and react to every event is shaped by all that has passed and will be influenced by all that is yet to come. We each have a unique interpretation of life!

A Mind for Life

Major life events have a way of significantly and rapidly changing the future. Losing one's eyesight in a car accident for example, will be the cause of reflection about all the ways that such loss would change everything. Many would be quick to declare it horrible and affirm that their life would never be the same again, with a negative connotation to it, of course. A rare few would express the intent to learn to see things differently and experience life in a new exciting way. A few others would be grateful for the amount of time during which they had their eyesight and vow to make the most of their days to come.

The reality is that unless this hypothetical person commits suicide, he or she will learn to adapt and live the best way possible.

You see, there are always many ways to view life events, favorably or negatively, and it really blows people's minds when we start discussing these concepts and they realize that they actually have choices, though frequently they make the wrong ones. You have two different people choosing to see their future differently and in large part self-determining how the rest of their lives will go. Since there are many options, you can now see how I might say one might unconsciously live a lie.

Have you ever really wondered what causes you to make the decisions you do? Have you knowingly and seemingly felt you should not do something, not stop only to proceed anyway and hurt yourself? Why is it we make such choices at times?

The notion of perspective is truly fascinating to examine. As a former part-time photographer, I was always intent on capturing my subjects from the right angle. When working with models I was always fascinated with how differently one could look in different poses and clothes, or even from just different angles. Also very interesting was how people seeing that model might think them completely different kinds of people from one picture to another.

Even more fascinating to me, though, was seeing how the models would perceive themselves, and which image of themselves would appeal to them personally. It often was the opinion of many people that the photos the models chose were the worst. Often others saw the models as better than the models saw their own self.

While this is all pretty subjective, whose opinion really matters? Well, in the photo business it's actually the audience, but to the models it's important how they see themselves. Two different vantage points of a possible countless number! Whose view is right and real?

Now, though large events can rapidly change our future, small ones are like water eroding and shaping mountains, and affect our thought processes and behavior just as deeply. Scientifically, when it comes to earth we refer to it as soil erosion, and since it tears things down, we generally give it a negative connotation, even though many of the great wonders we have today are a result of a process of erosion. Look at the Grand Canyon: it's after all the result of what many would deem negative forces!

With programming, if we touch a hot surface and feel pain our brain records and associates that experience with pain and makes a permanent brain note that touching similar surfaces will result in pain. Our mind will warn us of this cause and effect whenever we see hot surfaces and consider touching them.

In the case of a stove burner, we probably know not to touch it again after the first time. In other cases -- like with an oven plate, for example -- we learn to test the temperature before grabbing it.

When we consider all these small experiences, we realize that they shape the largest portion of our conscious behavior and thought process. They condition us to respond and behave in certain ways. The more conditioning we experience, the more predictable our behavior gets when future experiences come along.

Stopping to think about this process for a moment, you also need to understand that the more conditioned you get, the more difficult it is to break or override that programming. Drive down the same road 1000 times and see how hard it is to register the need to follow a detour without a sign forcing you to do so!

Why would we want to override our programming, though? Well, the problem with programming is, while it's usefulness is obvious when it comes to hot surfaces, it may not be obvious that this sort of programming also drives us to learn destructive, negative, bad behaviors and or responses and to hold negative beliefs.

Furthermore, these unconsciously learned patterns of behavior are weaved together like fibers in a rug and it becomes difficult to pull out just one fiber without impacting others. If each fiber represents a certain response, we can see that removing one that we feel is negative, might affect the good ones as well.

Sometimes our programming precludes us from being able to respond differently when we need it. Programming tends to be black and white, while life is very much a series of grey tones. Our conditioning therefore can limit our ability to adapt and roll with change.

A classic example would be two people who persistently do not get along. The very presence of the other causes each to become tense, change mood, and assume a more aggressive and hostile posture. You can see it in their body language and facial expressions.

People in this situation usually try to avoid each other, but in some cases there almost seems to be a sort of fatal attraction, so that instead of shunning each other, they actually seek interaction with each other.

You could ask each one of them point blank why they do not avoid the other person, and both would insist they do, and probably would pass a lie detector test. Still though, in reality they seek each other out and make themselves miserable. Why do they act this way instead of simply avoiding the emotional dismay their interaction causes? The problem is that although obvious, we often choose to ignore thoughts like these, and easily find faults in others while denying that we ourselves have many of the same faults.

However, sometimes we go beyond the blaming game and begin to question our own motives… How many times have you asked yourself, "Why do I keep doing this?" Or "Why can't I stop doing that?" Although that is a great first step, it's not enough in itself unfortunately. If you're willing to ask and just don't know how to get the answer, I might be able to help.

It might be easier to think about it this way. Imagine that one day you wake up and you find yourself feeling really strange, and don't understand what's going on with you. As your eyes adjust to the light and you are able to breathe easier, you see that there are wires hooked up to you everywhere. Eventually you realize that you were hooked up to a machine all your life, and that everything you knew, thought, and believed you experienced was all created by this machine. How would you feel?

What we do not realize is that this is pretty much how things really are, though without all the sci-fi drama and wires. Virtually speaking, you have been programmed and live your life in accordance with the programming of a virtual and invisible machine. I use the word machine liberally and symbolically as the machine represents all the external influences that embody the programming inside you. Yes, we are back to our evil puppet master again. And while it might seem totally insane, this is not always as bad as it sounds. Awareness and understanding that you can make your own choices is not as unconscious as simply just living out the programming you have been given.

Said another way, the programming gets 95% of people through each day, and they have little to no awareness or care about its existence. Depending on how we measure the quality of life, this process is successful in its own right and people can go on living this way for their entire lives.

So you might be asking once again at this point why should you care. Well, because in very basic terms, living a life that's been programmed for you can seem rather empty, lonely, and sometimes hollow. For some there are instances of happiness followed by many periods of disconnection from others, all that surround

The Mind

them, and even themselves. If you have ever felt this way, or still do, what I have described could be the very cause of it.

Let's see if I can provide an analogy. A friend bought you tickets to a killer event you have heard everyone hype up and which is supposed to be the event of a lifetime! You're extremely excited and can't wait! You count the days, hours and minutes with heated anticipation. Finally the moment arrives and you are there at this awesome event. Except, that it does not seem all that great and you begin to wonder why everyone made it out to be such a big deal! You are left feeling shortchanged, and yet you are pressured by your friends to say it was the event of all events! If you stopped and thought about it for a bit you might even reflect back and come to the conclusion that all the anticipation, preparation and talking about it with your friends was far more entertaining! Simple as those activities were, they were also in the end more fun. Enjoyment does not have to be an elaborate spectacle.

By now, while I have provided very few examples, you should be able to see that you are conditioned to respond and behave the way you do. The sum of your life experiences bring the state of conditioning to where you are here and now. Whether you are genetically predisposed (programmed) or your programming is learned, it can be modified, if you're willing to work at it.

Perhaps more of your conscious behavior and ideas are a lie than you might imagine. Ok, I'll go easy on you for now and just say that you should realize that at least part of how you act and feel is based on lies.

If you're making your own future then you are reprogramming and writing the script of your own life. Transcending the autopilot system where it matters will help you navigate towards a brighter, happier time. The events of the future, both big and small, will further shape and/or change your conditioning.

Think back and look at our diagram in the AM4L chapter again. If we gain awareness, then we can crack the system and reprogram. Remember the loop, the more awareness we gain, the more we can change our future behavior. The more we change our future behavior, the more we change our life experience. Our life experience impacts our conscious mind and our response to external stimuli.

Take a quick look back now… The mountains behind us are starting to show some distance! Turn around again now, and let's journey onward!

Frosty Trees
Mark Abraham
Gravel Road in Eudora, Kansas

I used to spend many hours out on the gravel roads not too far from where I lived. Just a few miles from the hustle and bustle of a busy community one can find views of crops, trees and other simple landscapes.

What you see here in this photo pales compared to what my eyes saw in the freezing cold. It was sunset and the colors were truly magical, glowing in the cold fog. There is so much to see and experience in this world, even in what many would consider a boring place like Kansas. Life is what we dare to make it, and if we do not venture much, then we end up with little.

Origins Of Programming

What are the origins of our programming? It's an excellent question and the answer is daunting. Stating that it comes from the sum of your experiences is too generic and high-level, so let's explore this idea in more detail.

From the second we leave the womb and enter the physical world we become self-aware, to a degree, and at that moment for certain, if not sooner, we feel the first sense of loss. Perhaps it is at that second that we also develop the desire to reject reality. We lose the warmth and shelter of the womb and enter the stark world of reality. When we awaken, literally or mentally, to this fact, we often begin to scream and cry, and while we are not likely to be able to really understand it, we probably wish we could return to the comfort of our mother's womb.

Birth also marks what I refer to the initiation of adaptive programming. When things become difficult in life, such finding ourselves in a cold, hard, bright new world, we adapt. It's funny that usually the negative things that we experience do not objectively change; it is us and the way we decide to deal with them that change. The world does not change when we are born, but we do, moment by moment. If something scares us, we learn not to be scared, if we're hungry or hurting we learn to deal with hunger and other forms of discomfort.

In this framing, adaptation is how I believe we begin to learn to unconsciously lie to ourselves in order to make things more rational and acceptable. Those around us begin to pass on their own rationalizations as well, and we ingest it all up with a voracious appetite because it provides an explanation for those things we do not understand. We suppress the pain and pacify ourselves with plausible explanations for the discomfort we experience. It's ironic that in reality we begin to reprogram ourselves right after birth to deal with the harshness of life itself.

Imagine, if you will, two men 4500 years ago watching the sun set… One man wonders where it went and the other begins to ponder it. During those times there was little science available to offer the type of explanation we have today. So they speculated, and when something sounded agreeable and plausible they went with it. This is how it goes with everything in life – We seek to find plausible answers more often than the truth. The more difficult a factual answer is to obtain, the more we theorize.

As time goes on, we begin to discern more of the facts and truth or at least we think of a better-designed rationalization for what we do not understand. In this above case, awareness was gained of how the tiny points of light in the sky moved in a pattern, and new theories emerged. Eventually we built telescopes and then spacecraft. We gained more facts and revised theories about the old questions, and then we found lots of new questions to replace them, and more new theories to answer these new questions.

Birth is also the initiation of self-centeredness! I can assure you at that very instant we are born we are thinking of no one else but ourselves, and our egocentrism will continue for many years. We want attention, we want love, and as we grow our wants will grow accordingly, our contentment with what we already have constantly weakens and is replaced by the desire for more. The more we come to know the more we come to want. If we fail to learn the value of others and care for them, then we become narcissistic and it could even lead to developing sociopathic tendencies.

Desire is really a black hole of sorts, and regrettably for many it often dictates their entire life! The want continues to grow and the sense of contentment further weakens. Material obtainment becomes our adaptation and a surrogate for our lack of spiritual development and understanding of why we are here. It's easier to handle and seemingly fills the spaces. While there are gaps, materialism keeps us busy and we can get so caught up in it that there is little time to question the confines of the box within which we force ourselves to live.

Often people frown at me when I say the more you want the less you'll have.

They tilt their heads and look at me like I'm insane. There is logic behind this simple, though seemingly absurd, statement. We are likely to get only about so much of all things in life, regardless of what they are. Let's take money for example... Few people become millionaires. A lot of people end up somewhere in the ranks of the middle class and have an average amount of money; and even more end up on the lower end of the scale and have little money, while some end up with barely enough to survive or not enough at all.

While it's true that the very rich might have all the money they could want in life, in the big picture this percentage of the population is quite small, (about 1-2%) and the concentration of wealth in this small portion of society leaves the larger middle and lower income groups with just a fraction of what the rich have.

Let's say for sake of this example that a rich person makes one million dollars a year, a middle-class person $100,000, and a poor person $20,000. If you are the poor person wanting a millionaire's life you will have just a tiny fraction of what you want, and if you aim for wanting a middle-class life you'll have 20% of what you want. If you just want to make $40,000 a year, you'll have half of what you desire. Please understand that this is a just an example, as I do realize that basic needs cost money and disposable income isn't a possibility for many until they make a certain amount of money.

Let's say now that we have a middle-class person that does not care about money all that much and who could easily and happily get by on $50,000 a year. Such person will believe he or she has more than needed with their $100,000 income, while another person with the same income who covets a millionaire's life will constantly feel unsatisfied. If you desire what a $50,000 a year buys you and you make $100,000 a year, you'll likely have all you materially want, and so on. Ironically, you also have millionaires who are not content because they want to be billionaires. You may have heard the saying, "You can never have too much!" I'd counter it as follows: "You'll never be happy no matter how much you have!"

The dynamics of desire is why the more you want the less you'll have -- It's really a matter of perspective and levels of need. Earlier on I have said that life is a lie, and maybe now you can see in what context I made this statement. The more you want the less you'll have is a truth.

Now, let's take a moment to think about the different ways people are programmed when it comes to wants. Think about phrases you may have heard since childhood:

- Aim for the stars and you'll hit the moon!
- Take what's there for the taking or someone else will!
- It's a dog-eat-dog world and the meanest dog eats!
- You have to push and shove your way to the top!
- Never take what is not yours!
- Humility is a noble quality!

Consider the people that are likely to say these things to you and what motivates them to say them. You'll realize that many of the people referenced above in the different social classes we described in monetary terms were probably influenced by some of these teachings.

I am not advocating or denouncing any of the statements above – They are simply emblematic of different belief systems. Some work for people and some do not. Personally I'd think that none of them has much to do with the reality and meaning of life, and I believe that true happiness and peace is not really materially bound, though we have been largely programmed to connect happiness with the material world.

So our programming in part comes from our parents, our teachers, ministers, TV, radio, peers, leaders, good people, bad people, in summary, all kinds of people; and, as previously discussed, it also comes from the sum of our life experiences, which obviously encompasses all the people above mentioned. Finally, a large part of it comes from our own selves as a result of our adaptation and of how we choose to view those experiences.

These events and people shape our belief systems and responses to future events. As we go through life we learn and subscribe to theories, and then form beliefs or programs. To some extent, unless you become aware of these programs, you are destined to respond in a predetermined way by virtue of the program's execution.

This is why awareness is key to becoming the master of your current and future encoding. Not all of it is negative, and as I mentioned earlier, we also program ourselves to explain what we cannot easily understand. Rationalization feels better than emptiness, and it's at least a step toward answering the unexplained. Awareness enables us to simply be more conscious in the selection of our future responses, so that we are programming our future behavior and thoughts in a more positive, constructive manner.

I guess I would be remiss if I failed to talk about the cultural aspects of programming. Whether you are a tribe member that watches the sun and moon and bases your decisions on their rising and setting or you're a scientist at NASA who peers into the depths of the farthest reaches of the cosmos and ponders creation, the

Origins Of Programming

cultural foundation on which you stand, which is rooted in your beliefs, is essential to your ability to survive. Each person – and each culture -- has a framework within which they structure their answers.

I admit I might have set you up earlier, playing on the idea that your life is a lie! To be honest, reality is something that is very subjective, and whether we ever truly experience it might be irrelevant for most. I am not suggesting that your mission become seeking the real meaning of life, or even that finding the truth about your own life be the end goal. On my part, this journey of discovery is ultimately about finding greater happiness through awareness.

Life is like a car with a tank of gas. We fill that tank and we have to decide how to best use the fuel. We can drive around and think about it or we can pre-plan our route to somewhere exotic and special, but I do not think either is right. You get forced to start driving the minute you're pushed out into life, and it's all about not turning down so many wrong and useless streets while becoming a savvy driver, since we are not really allotted much time to plan.

Awareness is not something easily cultivated, yet there is a secret to achieving it! To really obtain *A Mind For Life* you have to master this one key mental ability, Awareness. We'll keep talking about it as we move through this book. It's so simple and yet so very difficult to harness. You have to believe that you can gain greater awareness, but most importantly, you need to possess the desire to develop it.

Don't look up or back yet, let's walk some more!

The Way We See Things

"You have probably often heard that the quality of our life is often dictated by the choices we make. Of even greater relevance are the consequences of how we choose to view the events of our life and the enormous impact this decision has on our happiness."

I am reminded of a moment some years ago while driving to work. I had been working on a project for a few years and had been averaging 78 hours a week for its duration. At work people would look at me and I would see the pity in their eyes. So there I was in my car, the sun just rising above the trees, the rays gloriously slashing the morning sky, and the grass dewy and glistening. It was all very much like one of those images with beams of light pouring down to earth from heaven!

A Mind for Life

While most people would have been down and out, I was strangely proud that morning… I felt triumph in being able to survive such a long haul, sort of like running a long marathon! I've always tried to keep things in perspective, and while most people around me thought me a poor overworked mule, I tempered my situation with the thought of people far worse off in the world, homeless, hungry, beaten, weary, persecuted, etc. There I was, though, proud to be a survivor and basking in this magnificent morning in spite of three consecutives weeks of 110, 112, and even 120 work hours, as that last one had been.

We were delivering our project later than its deadline, so though we were nearing the finish, our effort was nonetheless generally considered a failure. As a team we had to look within ourselves and know we had poured all we had into this project. It was hard to have spent all those hours and feel that we had failed. The human spirit is truly amazing and it is in this spirit that I offer perspective and also caution to you. While we can become proud of our toughness, we may also want to reflect on the stupidity of signing up for and persisting in something that leads us to need to be so tough.

In the last chapter I talked about how the mind works, about programming and overcoming it. Not all the challenges we face can be directly tied to mere programming, but we can use the same techniques to examine our thoughts and emotional responses so we can modify and learn from them whenever needed.

In this example I had signed up for an impossible mission and willingly subjected myself to a form of torture. Nobody was really consciously torturing me -- I was torturing my own self. I justified it in many ways: essential to my job, a chance to learn and get ahead, and a way to bring about positive change. Furthermore, I was convinced that if I refused, they would find someone else who would accept. But what would have happened if I had instead explored reasons to say no, such as health, marriage, time, happiness, just to name a few?

There were two paths I could have followed, each with its own consequences. My choice impacted my marriage and my health (I gained a lot of weight during that experience and destroyed my sleep cycle as well), it caused me to endure extreme grief and disappointment, and ultimately changed my entire future.

This work experience, combined with the two previous years, left a 5-year hole in my life I call "the coma." Literally, I was very much not present to myself in those years. I stopped doing most of the things I enjoyed, missed major news events and complete TV series, you name it… It was all a black hole. There are so many ways to see things and it can be very difficult to process all data and make correct decisions.

A long time has passed since then, but I still discover things I completely bypassed during those years. For example, I was so far gone that although I recall watching a particular TV series on DVD during that period in my rare spare time, that when I went to share that same series with my wife I was amazed at how much I had totally forgotten. I remember really liking it, but whenever she'd ask me what was going to happen next, I realized I had no idea. She thought I was just teasing her, but, sadly, I was not.

Many people would blame others for these negative experiences; I blame myself and take accountability for everything. It was ultimately my choices that led to it all. Strangely enough, while

A Mind for Life

I would have liked to gain the knowledge in an easier way, considering how minds function, I would not want to go without the understanding I gained from it. Today I look at it that period with a very different set of eyes!

It is partly to this concept of new eyes that I have been leading you. The answer to the meaning of life is simply that life is truly what you make it. You have choices, and while you may not be able to control everything that happens or be wise enough to make all the right choices, you will always retain your ability and right to choose how you wish to see your life and the people around you, and to find your own way to interpret it all. Your adaption, rationalization and understanding of your experiences will give life a meaning that is unique to your being -- Another person who has been at your side and been part of the same events may have in fact a completely different interpretation.

I do a lot of thinking when driving, as I'm sure you have noticed. I was going to Minnesota to see my father with my present wife and love of my life and talking to her about photography. I handed her my camera and asked her to take a picture. The lens was at its widest setting so it would capture the largest swath of landscape wherever she pointed the camera. I then asked her to take another photo, but this time zoomed in all the way. I had her look at the difference between the images, and explained that while every day we walk around and see things in real size, there are different ways to observe the world around us in larger and smaller scales. I told her that before I really got into astronomy I hardly ever looked up at the night sky and noticed the stars. I also talked about how things looked through a telescope and how, with a lot of magnification, I could see galaxies that were millions and millions of light years away, otherwise completely invisible to the naked eye. The notion of scale goes unconsidered by many and it's unfortunate, because there is so much to see all around us. When was the last time you really took a good look around?

This point of view variance also applies to how we see weather, and for that matter, to all the occurrences in our life! Do you see a storm as bad, dreary and dark or as a phenomenon to be witnessed and viewed with awe or appreciation, just like a sunny day? I am not suggesting there is a right or wrong answer -- While I personally might view a storm as exciting and humbling, it may just be a horribly scary event in someone else's world. The point, though, is that the choice is yours to make, and that by making different choices we can see things more positively and with a greater level of happiness.

The choices we make shape the reality in which we live. Making different choices allows us to travel down different paths. It's not that our lives are all a big lie, we shouldn't think about it that way. The important thing to remember is that we get to choose.

Back to my previous story, the hardship I experienced was, to me, a hardship. While not comparable to mayhem and starvation, it was a major event in my life. I had a misplaced notion that hard work and dedication always resulted in success. Going through this hardship, however, removed me of this notion, taught be a valuable lesson, and changed my life for the better. Today, I feel fortunate to have learned what I did and only be in my forties. I'll never look at life the same way again and that is a good thing!

We can be proud of how tough we are. At the same time, however, we should view our experiences with an equal amount of humility for our stupidity. This will allow us to learn from our life experiences and shape a better future to come!

Are you beginning to see things from more than one vantage point? What's the best angle?

Earlier I spoke of being hooked up to a machine: the machine controlling your experiences and drawing out your life's storyboard. Do you remain hooked up? Do you believe you are symbolically hooked to a machine that's driving your life? Does the thought make you uncomfortable? Is the entire notion of this annoying?

I'm asking you a lot of questions but what I am really suggesting is simply a partial decoupling from the machine. For many of us the machine does a pretty decent job of getting us through life. Developing A Mind For Life is about selectively pulling a few wires off and regaining manual control over some parts of our lives. If we look at it as a partial, rather than total, removal from the machine it's easier to deal with. If you buy the notion that something other than yourself is running your life, the thought of cutting all the cords could be scary.

A Mind For Life will not make all of your problems go away. It will, however, alter the virtual machine's performance to output more happiness. In terms of adaptive thinking, what I am suggesting is that we tune up the machine to allow us to adapt and live our lives in a friendlier, more compatible, and happier way.

Let's delve deeper and see if we can ease your fears and answer more of your questions.

Remember, it's all about the way you see things. Look up! Are those mountains looking a little closer now? Don't look back yet!

Sotol Morning
Mark Abraham
Big Bend National Park Texas 2006

The sun emerged from the horizon casting color and light across the landscape and its warmth raised our spirits! A drive through the fog before the sun started to rise. I sipped on some freshly made instant coffee! It was delicious on this morning, despite being instant!

When did you last witness the sun rising and how did you feel? Maybe it's time to catch one!

Life Cycles

For most people, life is based on cycles. Since most of us go through a similar emotional evolution, these cycles, or life phases, are fairly predictable. My identification of the latter phases is more from observation than actual experience since, given my age, I cannot yet have possibly experienced them all myself.

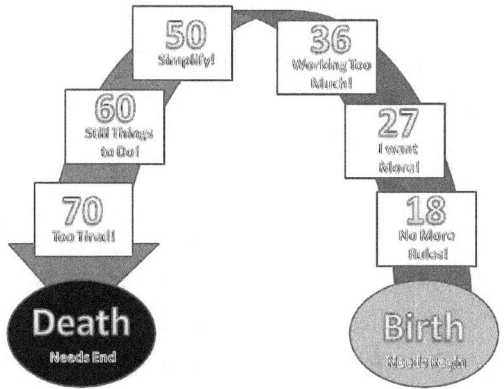

A Mind for Life

The illustration above generalizes the cycles I have chosen to discuss at a very high level. Let's dive into them in a little deeper.

The ages you see are not an exact science. Whether due to our life experiences or our genetic wiring, some of us go through these changes at a younger age while others experience them later in life. Others may not experience them at all.

Additionally, these phases are not a complete representation of the cycles we experience in a lifetime. There are several developmental phases that occur in childhood. I have elected, however, to start at age 18 and focus on the particular milestones I feel are the most relevant to the overall message of this book.

Why am I covering this? Simply because life is somewhat cyclic and often follows a predictable pattern. Understanding this pattern ahead of time has value. It's also interesting that, to a large extent, the human experience employs a common set of programs and results in similar life experiences. This validates the notion of mass programming.

I am not suggesting you buck the cycle and skip phases. To do so would be against our very nature. The funny thing about life is that, despite our best efforts, most of us have a burning need to learn lessons the hard way, first hand, regardless of how many times we are told and shown.

Sometime around age 18 we are ready to leave the nest. Tired of the rules that exist at home and believing we are capable of making our own decisions we set off to college, join the military, start working full-time, or some variation or combination of these things. Some of us are kicked out the door by our parents.

Life Cycles

What we didn't know at the time was how often life would humble us, that we would need to make and follow our own rules to be successful and that having to work for a living was going to take up much more of our time than we expected.

Sometime around age 27 many of us think we figure things out. Often this is when we finally choose and/or settle into our career. We start to embrace our occupation more closely and consequently kick our efforts up a notch. We realize that working harder and climbing the corporate ladder will help us get more of the things we believe we need in order to be happy. Events such as buying a house, getting married, having children, and sometimes ending a bad marriage act as catalysts, propelling us forward with more intensity. Some of us, particularly the slow starters, find ourselves going back to school or learning new skills.

What we didn't know at the time is that all the money in the world can't buy happiness. I know some of you out there will disagree. But consider this: If you had one month to live, how long would a billion dollars keep you happy? The rest of your life? I smile as I write this because spending all that money in one month will probably become a chore and a distraction from creating truly meaningful moments in your final days of life. Do you really believe a giant shopping spree will make dying easier? I am guessing that spending some quality time with those you love most will bring yor more peace and comfort and provide you with that final spiritual boost we all need in order to face death.

Additionally, we often fail to realize that we can become a slave to the material things that we were programmed to desire so very, very much!

A Mind for Life

After several years of hard work, sometime around age 36-45 we realize that maybe we are working too hard and not enjoying life enough. We get a midlife fever which shakes our beliefs, making us wish we were young again and had a chance to do some things over. Sometimes we realize it's not too late and so we change directions a bit. At this point we either regress and go a little crazy chasing after our youth or we decide to mellow out, simplify, and carve out more time for ourselves. Some of us even do a little of both.

What we didn't know at the time is that our youth was not so special; it was full of silly, meaningless events that often didn't make any sense. Eventually, we quit chasing our youth, embrace getting older, and move on to the next phase of our life.

Depending how the previous phase went at this age, sometime in between ages 44-55 we be decide to simplify and focus more on the end game. This includes securing retirement and thinking more seriously about where we want to live when we retire.

For many people, this phase is also the post-children period. With the children gone, they learn to work with their new found freedom, perhaps engaging more in the things they enjoy hobbies, home projects, higher learning, and an increased focus on health. Additionally, we often begin to feel the aches and pains associated with getting older as we wake and work through each day.

I won't elaborate much on the later phases as I haven't personally experienced them myself. I will say that sometime in our fifties many people become more serious and focused on their retirement. Often we also experience a kind of cleansing: clearing out things we don't use, letting go of junk, and losing our attachment to sentimental objects. We may also get more serious and committed to our spiritual beliefs.

At some point we retire and want to relax. During this phase many of us learn to make do with less stuff. We realize that retirement is more expensive than we thought and that our life of leisure may be more focused on rest than world travel. We also learn how well we really planned and in some cases realize we still need to work longer than we thought.

Finally, we learn to relax, reflect and, as our facilities begin to evaporate, we stop fighting and begin to embrace the final chapter of our life. Some welcome the slow march toward death while others greet it with bitterness and regrets. This may sound harsh, however, it is often all too real!

Sure, many people's lives don't strictly adhere to the model I have described. In fact, regardless of reading this book, your life will continue to have many of the same events it does today. It is the choices you make in response to these events that are really being discussed in the picture.

It is interesting that throughout our lives we often revisit those areas we either felt we could have or needed to managed better.

A lot of this book talks about the underlying programming instilled in each of us as we go through life that drives much of what I have described. We can shorten some of the negativity if we are aware of the path we are on when we first start walking it.

It is better to get halfway down a path, realize you're on the wrong trail and turn around than it is to get to the end of the path and you have walk the entire way back. Understanding how you feel and what you believe today may change tomorrow.

With the economy the way it is here in 2010 as I write this, the timing of learning to expect and want less is valuable. You might find that reading this book in your late thirties or forties may have the most impact. If you're younger you can make changes and gain awareness earlier and spare yourself a lot of grief. I started in my late twenties and really started working it hard in my thirties. If you are older you can gain some clarity and validation and still make changes if needed.

We have been marching a bit now: look up, look ahead! Can you see a little more detail in the mountains ahead? Don't look back yet!

Fountain
Mark Abraham
The Plaza, Kansas City Missouri 2006

One fine morning I ventured out early and experienced the city as the sun was just rising. I had the streets to myself and just walked - taking in the sights and sounds of the empty cobblestone streets.

This photo captures my memory of that morning well. I took a little time to just stand, watch and listen to a simple fountain in the early morning light!

A School Play

Becoming a new parent has exposed me to a diverse array of people and a renewed insight into the world today's children inhabit. As I drove home from an evening spent with family at a school play another insight into reality struck me.

We spend much of our life being unaware of parts of ourselves because we haven't yet experienced some aspect of life that reveals them to us. I had this revelation on the way home that night.

As we watched the play I began to wonder if my stepdaughter was hoping her real father would be there to see her perform! It's amazing how quickly we can feel and transverse so many emotions in mere seconds and minutes. An array of emotions flashed through me with blinding speed. Our mind must process these feelings at light speed and, sometimes, during this process a new piece of ourselves is revealed.

I don't know that I can convey what it's like to be given the gift of step-daughters so late in my life. Having never been a father before, even after spending a year as a parental figure, I learn and have new experiences each day.

The pain I felt when I realized she would be longing for her real father as opposed to me showed me how much I cared for her. It is akin to being unaware you're in love and then realizing your true feelings when that person breaks your heart. Of course she didn't mean to hurt me, nor is she at any fault for how I felt in that moment.

Quickly my self-centered emotions changed into recognition of the possible despair and heartbreak of a young girl hoping to see her father. She unconsciously experiences this over and over again, knowing that 98 out of 100 times he will not arrive. Regardless, her hope that he will is never ending. If you ever thought your impact was insignificant as a parent with regards to showing up to your children's big moments, think again!

You see, for me and for my own father, I think unconsciously I always hoped he would show up and that it would have the power to erase all that had passed before; he would simply be my father again. If you ever wondered about love and the capacity to forgive, look no further than this example.

It may not be logical; it's simply how it is for children who find themselves with a parent that is alive and out there but is mostly absent in their life.

A School Play

It's worse when you realize that your parent is not even making much effort to change. It leaves a terrible emptiness inside that child and I found myself being that child over and over again throughout my life with my own father's impact upon me and my life.

I sometimes believe this is why I am in these girls lives now, to help them sort through what took me so many years to comprehend. There are moments, however, where we as adults feel helpless, because what a young girl wants is what she wants, and there are no real substitutes or pacifiers for her desires. Explaining it all would only make it worse and dash her misplaced hopes.

I think my father's passing has, in part, helped me come to terms with it. With the new gift of these girls in my life, however, I do see them facing potentially similar challenges and am virtually helpless most times to wipe that pain away.

I try to be the best father figure I can and be there for them unconditionally, while still maintaining some semblance of being a role model and real father figure. I have no expectations for what I try to offer and give and do not expect them to appreciate or care that I do. I try to make the love I have for them as unconditional as I can. It's not always easy and I am not always successful, but I do try to make a difference and hope to make an impact!

Again, if you ever believe being there for your child doesn't really matter, think again!

Paola Line

Mark Abraham
Paola, Kansas 2006

I looked across the yard at the empty can of spam in the pile of what was surely leftover from a homeless man's night. I felt a pang of loneliness and a hint of nostalgia for days and times past.

I looked down into the distance and the sun shown upon the empty rails on the left and the active rails on the right. I wondered when the next train would pass and where it would be destined!

It's just an old rail yard, but it generated feelings, and when we feel we are moved, we are living and we become one with everything. Even rusty train rails on a late fall afternoon can cause a person to feel connected!

Truth And Integrity

I believe integrity is huge! You have probably been taught about the virtues of integrity many times. How karma, for instance, will take its toll should you live a life with weak and/or deficient integrity.

I realize many people think karma is a bunch of bull. Many of us look at bad or evil people who step on countless others yet live rich, live high and never seem to pay a price for their behavior. I, however, do believe their bad behavior comes at a cost!

Have you ever come across a person or business that was a pure pleasure to deal with? You walked away from them feeling they were forthright, that they delivered on their word even when there were issues, that they treated you with courtesy and respect, and finally that they were notably honest? My chiropractor is always like that, she strives to make sure I leave fully adjusted, even if it takes a while and I give her a hard time. It feels good to work with professionals, doesn't it?

I believe integrity is more important to our own sense of balance than it is to the people with whom we interact. You might ask how that can be and the answer is very short and simple. I believe you must be able to look in the mirror and feel good about yourself. Ultimately, self-image is created when we look at ourselves in the mirror and see the way we act, behave, think and treat others. We then live as we see and feel about ourselves. Often the psychological ramifications of our image unconsciously affect our behavior. This means that even if we smile at ourselves, our subconscious is living and breathing a life of its own, and it may have a very different view of you than your conscious self does.

Some call it consciousness; others call it karma; and others call it the soul. If you do not care about your own integrity, you'll never sincerely value it in others. Karma is not simply about how you treat others. In large part, it is about feeling good about your own behavior and radiating that good feeling to everyone you come in contact with.

Maybe the easiest way to elaborate is to say: If you live life with integrity you may not please all people, however, you will likely please yourself.

Acting and living with integrity can sometimes makes others uncomfortable since they may struggle with the work or effort that is often required to do it themselves. They may also not have strong self-images. You can often be seen as a do-gooder or someone that simply makes life difficult for others. Many people work hard at not being seen as "goody-two-shoes". It's ironic that often living with integrity carries such a burden. Of course, one must work to maintain balance and not take it too far.

Let's walk through some examples! Consider, for instance, a stereotypically lazy person. They don't like to work; they do everything they can to get out of working, even at surprising costs. Often this leads to lies. Lies are betrayals to the people to whom we tell them. They are also demonstrative of a lack of trust or an unwillingness to let people see who we really are and how we really think. They are also indicative of low self-esteem. If we are able to be seen and accept the consequences of who we are then lies aren't necessary.

Lazy people tend to believe it's okay to have other people do their work for them. At the same time, when they are narcissistic about it they look down on others and often consider these people to be fools and/or petty individuals. They grow complacent and become comfortable shunning their responsibilities. They continue to be lazy without suffering any consequences for the behavior.

A lazy mentality can further cause the mind and thought process to degrade to a point that when laziness does have consequences, often lazy people hold others responsible and blame them for their own failings. The more this occurs, the more comfortable and easy it becomes to avoid accountability. More often than not, these people dig both physical and moral holes for themselves. They often fail to comprehend how deep they have dug themselves in as they find themselves further and further down the hole.

Integrity plummets as a person passes through this bleak cycle of failing to help others, not shouldering their own responsibilities, lying to avoid difficulty, believing they are better than others and failing to take accountability for their actions. These are all attributes associated with weak or absent integrity.

This is also a form of adaptation and self-programming. We don't like feeling judged or experiencing the consequences of our poor character. This leads many people to feel guilt, depression and low self-esteem. Often people fail to see the connection between poor behavior and feelings of inadequacy. If, however, they do make the connection they either choose to repair their behavior and change their narcissistic character or they find a plausible way to bury it, ignore it and allow their behavior to continue. The more indifference they have towards others the more sociopathic they become.

It's fascinating to watch a person like this who is in total denial of their true self. Unfortunately, many people don't recognize these sociopaths until it's too late and they have victimized them. You can meet a very sociopathic person and not even realize it for a long time. They seem nice, hold prominent titles in society, and look you right in the eye while lying to you and considering how they are going to use you without feeling a speck of guilt or remorse.

Integrity for the sake of placing yourself above others can be equally bad and also reap bad consequences. It leads to believing one is elite and this superiority leads to exclusion and ultimately loneliness for many. Be very careful not to use your newfound awareness to establish your superiority over others. If you believe yourself better then you essentially initiate another type of narcissistic program. It is better to think of it as if you're simply following a different path. Keep in mind that there are people that live seemingly happy programmed lives. Awareness to them may even generate depression.

If you are not careful then you will be seen only as a do-gooder rather than a great person that people want to be associated with. To frequently judge others and hold a double standard also weakens a person's integrity. You can begin to feel as if nobody is good enough to keep your company. As you can imagine, balance can and often is difficult to achieve.

Let's walk through another thought pattern.

We treat people with dignity, respect them without judgment, value their differences, and even embrace their shortcomings. We don't consider ourselves to be superior to others and are always willing to consider ideas with an open mind. We see ourselves neither above nor below others.

We lead by example, treating others fairly and upholding our principles. We examine our principles regularly and acknowledge there are sometimes exceptions to our values. We seek to bring about change through influence. We understand that sometimes our principles may be unpopular and unaccepted by others. We try to bring integrity into a positive light. We understand and accept others may simply be different and our ability to affect change is, although noble, limited. We seek to inspire change through influence and education and not through force or coercion. We strive to find a common higher ground to bring people together rather than work to divide and conquer. We realize that our own wants and needs may have a lower place in the big picture! We ask questions and do not make accusations and convictions.

A Mind for Life

How does this model sound to you at a high-level?

We see ourselves neither above them, below them nor as equals to them.

I highlight this phrase because it's of paramount importance. You have probably been told many times not to place yourself above others. You have probably also been told not to place yourself beneath others. Instead, you are told to believe yourself equal and worthy in life.

So what does it mean when I say you are not equal? To me, this statement means that I try not to think or compare people. I try to accept that people are all different and that these differences are what make people interesting. I also believe that everyone has their own path and is part of the larger social and emotional eco-system. I have thought about it long and hard and have come to the conclusion that comparing people leads to generating expectations. I believe we all just are. I am not saying, however, that bad people will always be bad and good people will always be good.

I am suggesting that bad people are essential to our emotional development and building our overall character. It is through the pain they inflict that we grow. Without bad in life there is no notion of good. It's not a complex notion; it simply is how it is. In nature there are predators and prey. Things get very unpredictable when the numbers get out of balance.

I realize this may sound more like a sermon than open thoughts on integrity. Personal integrity empowers us to be true, to look others in the eye, to treat people with dignity and thus to keep our overall lives less complicated and easier to manage. Corporate integrity is also important. Hard work and integrity, more often than not, pay out significantly more than the alternatives.

It's also funny how much energy and effort people sometimes expend while trying to avoid hard work. Their lies require more lies and lead others to lose trust in them. Overall support for these people diminishes. Once they have lost their support and integrity, others view and treat them differently. I believe, ultimately, it leads to a harder life.

If you can't grasp it spiritually, embrace it as a measure of just being plain smart! As you grow spiritually you'll find that the virtues of leading a good life manifest themselves in many more smiles and happiness.

Perhaps the hardest part of maintaining integrity is facing and overcoming the feelings that inevitably come when you are acting with integrity and others are not. You can experience anger, frustration and even hate!

I have found that treating people with integrity often drives them to act with integrity. It's about laying out a clear path for them to follow, brightly coloring the lines and marking the boundaries. If you show people that the only way they can deal with you is with integrity, they will either follow your example or avoid dealing with you at all! Crafted correctly, those with integrity do not even see the construct while those that lack integrity struggle to stay between the lines.

We can use our powers of observation, intuition and common sense to determine when we need to make clear the boundaries of the integrity we operate from within. One program I have written and tried to implement in life is called the STUPID program. It simply goes like this.

Can someone ask me if I am stupid based on the level of trust or assumptions I have made?

Consider, for example, that you lent a stranger a key to your house. If you came home and found it empty and the police asked you what happened, would you feel stupid? It would be hard to explain why you gave your key to a complete stranger. Duh, right?

We have to work on the balance between trust, expectations and paranoia. Sometimes, when we find ourselves working and dealing with people who do not behave with integrity and seemingly never will, then a different approach is required. The easiest approach is to deal with them as little as possible or, better yet, not at all.

If you must, however, then it is best to make sure you have a written agreement that provides for a tangible legal remedy. It is important to create consequences for venturing outside the lines.

The main point here isn't so much about others as it is about us. An honest life is a good life. It's also a more spiritually complete life. When I speak about spirituality, I am referring to all people, including those who practice religion and those who do not.

Spirituality exists at many levels and in many forms. If spirituality were represented as a pyramid, then our consciousness might appear on the bottom building block, layered with awareness, then inner spirituality and oneness with God on top.

Truth And Integrity

When we deal with truth in ourselves and with others these blocks all stack up to a much happier position in life. This is what karma is: peace within us and thus peace with others. Karma isn't about how you treat others; it's the core feeling within yourself about how you see yourself treating others. It's about how you feel about yourself and your position towards others. If that spirit within you is rich and strong then others will consider you to have strong karma.

How It's All About Me

I have talked about self-centeredness many times throughout this book. Self interest is often both our greatest strength and our greatest weakness. I wrote this chapter to sell you on just how into yourself you really are. That may seem harsh, however it's critical to understand in developing awareness and A Mind For Life.

You might argue about how much you think of others, how much you care and how much you give. If you do then you're proving my point. A better argument would be to say nothing and simply listen for a while.

You see, we wear a set of glasses that mostly blind us to the rest of the world. When we meet or talk to another person our thoughts often focus on how WE feel about them and not how they feel about us or their own lives. We are tremendously biased to look at everything from our own perspective.

For example, suppose you give a gift to someone and you can't wait to see their reaction to it! The giving of the gift is about you and your need for that reaction. Yes, you care about how they feel but you are expecting and wanting a reaction and that is for you. It's funny how disappointed you will get if they don't react the way you expect or desire. If you consider your own experiences with gifting in this context you can see how much about YOU those gifts really were.

It's this way with friendships as well. We expect our friends to listen and often we respect them by listening to them in return as well. How much of this is really about talking at the other person rather than talking with them. I have seen so many people wish for the other person to hurry up and finish speaking so they can relay their own stories, views and opinions. Friendships are often very selfish. If you add it all up, in terms of percentiles, most of our friendships are self-centered. It's very rare to make a connection with someone that is completely two-sided.

As a side bar, stop and think for a minute! How many real conversations do you have with others verses conversations where you just speak, feel good that you have had your say without regard as to whether your words were truly heard or even processed or understood? How well do you really listen to and seek to understand and seek to have empathy for others?

Let's look at it from a different angle! Let's say you have ten friends. Let's also say that by default you are focused on yourself about 50% of the time. This leaves another 50% to allocate to your

How It's All About Me

friends. Let's assume that in those friendships you try to employ a true 50/50 give and take rule. This means that of the 50% you had to allocate your friendships, 25% of that will be focused solely on yourself. That leaves only 25% of yourself to give to your friends. This is a very generous view of things. In reality, we usually focus less than 10% of ourselves on others.

At this point you may be questioning what all of this really means.

The reason I am taking you down this path is because your sense and need for self represents a huge influencing factor in the way your life plays out. Most of us realize that, at a minimum, we need to present ourselves as caring and attentive people in order to make others see and treat us well. Sooner or later, however, your true nature and desires will shine through. All of your efforts to present yourself well will be for naught and, even worse, you will not be perceived to be a genuine person. This leads to its own set of consequences.

Some people assert that they simply don't care all that much about others. They accept and acknowledge their self-centeredness and are not really willing to change. I applaud you at this point for your honesty and self-recognition. If this is your outlook, however, you should not expect to be treated like a better person than who you really are.

What about your spirit and your soul? What does it mean for YOU? Since you are focused entirely on yourself, this concern should be near and dear to your heart! I could attempt to guilt you into wanting to be a better person by calling you heartless, shallow, and countless other negative adjectives. Bah Humbug right? Three ghosts later you awake to turn over a new leaf in life! I know, I know! Smile!

We both know though that most of the time it's simply not going to work that way. So now what? Let's focus on a more spiritual plane. I can't force you to accept it or make you live on that plane. It's something you have to want and, yes, work for! The more self-centered you are, the harder it is climb your way onto that plane. If you're not religious put the notion of God aside and focus on the idea of harmony.

If you have ever felt as if you're riding in the groove and life feels sweet and smooth then you'll understand what existing on that plane is like. This alone would be a major incentive for wanting to change, as it is a truly wonderful feeling to exist with everyone and everything in greater harmony. Focusing on others more often allows you to achieve this increased harmony. There is a form of enlightenment that is imparted when we arrive and live on this higher plane more frequently.

For more depth on all this, look for the chapters on Caring and The Path. When you arrive at the end of this book, explanations of the true rewards of awareness and simplified living will become more evident.

So Frustrating

Why is my life so frustrating and annoying?

The very short answer to this question is simple: because you allow it to be that way. I am certain you aren't happy with this answer. Let me explain my reasoning, however, and see if it makes more sense and is more relatable.

The easiest way to illustrate my point is to provide you with some examples.

I talked to this gentleman one time; he was very annoyed because people wouldn't respect his lunch hour. They called him while he was eating, sent meeting requests scheduled during his lunch hour, and randomly dropped by his office while he was eating lunch. According to this gentleman, all he wanted in his work life was to have an undisturbed lunch hour.

I asked him why he accepted calls and meeting invitations during his lunch hour. He shrugged his shoulders and tilted his head. "I don't know," he answered.

I asked him what he thought would happen if he didn't answer his phone during lunch. He replied that he believed they would leave a message or call back another time.

I asked him what would happen if he didn't accept meeting requests scheduled during his lunch hour and he responded that they would probably reschedule the meeting for another time.

I asked him what would happen if he shut his door during lunch and he responded that people would probably come back later.

This is a classic example of how we allow ourselves to get frustrated and annoyed. Much of the time it's our own doing.

Why is bill paying time so annoying? Perhaps it's because we have not setup auto-pay for our bills. Maybe it's because we have many services that we continue to pay for and don't really even use or need. Do you really read that magazine to which you subscribe? How about that coffee of the month club, are you really enjoying it, do you use it enough to get that big discount they promised?

Why does my computer crash all the time? What operating system are you using? I have been amazed at how much better my life got by switching to a Mac. Nope, nobody paid me for this advertisement, it's just my experience. I feel like I have far fewer problems and get a lot more work done.

So Frustrating

Buy better products and you'll have fewer problems. Buy fewer things and there will be less headaches. How many handy dandy kitchen gadgets do you have: a blender, a juicer and a food processor? Why not simplify and buy one machine that does it all? Maybe I should try selling appliances rather than peace of mind, huh? Smile!

You probably get the point by now. This is a classic example of how you'll need to apply this type of questioning and logic in order to root out all the things in life that are causing you pain.

Here's the million dollar secret!

If you train yourself to STOP and ask, "Why am I feeling this way?" whenever you experience negative feelings and emotions, you will learn a lot about yourself and why you are often your own worst enemy. The key is to accept responsibility for the things that bother you. By developing the mental acuity to interrupt yourself as you start down the negative feelings rabbit-hole, you will be 1000 times closer to achieving A Mind For Life!

Let's revisit our discussion about self-accountability. In case you are questioning this reasoning, let me provide a clarifying example. Assume someone is bullying or treating you poorly.

You might say, well, how can I be responsible for that victimization? Instead, I encourage you to think about it like this: "Why are you allowing yourself to be bullied? Why are you even around this person? How did they get into your life? Why must they remain in your life? What can I (me) do, to stop it?"

A Mind for Life

A lot of bad things happen to us in life due to our own poor design! If you can't get a job because you don't have a college degree, it's not anyone else's fault but your own. Nothing will change until you make the change.

If you can't stop and take time to think ahead and make better decisions, then try and learn to stop and think it over as you begin to experience pain and frustration. The key is to gain awareness in the moment and call a timeout on yourself. It takes practice! Make a reminder device that you'll run into 5 times a day prompting you to stop and think when anger or frustration starts. Look on the AM4L website for a free downloadable sticker kit of AM4L stickers you can print out and make yourself.

Put it on a sticky atop your alarm clock. That way, when you go to turn off the alarm, it's the first thing you see. Put another on your front door so you see it on the way out of the house. Leave one on your monitor at work so you run into it while you are working.

See a recurring point of pain in almost every day? That is the perfect place to leave the sticky. It will remind you that that feeling is just a part of daily life and it shouldn't ruin your day.

The more you simplify life, the easier it will get. Learn to live debt free and you'll sleep a whole lot better at night. The key is to not complicate your life. Avoid adding complexity to your life. This is a trap we fall into frequently.

Consider the example of buying a fancy juicer because every once in a while you need to squeeze an orange. This makes me laugh even thinking about it because your frustration will change from the act of squeezing the orange to the effort that's required to

So Frustrating

clean the juicer when you're done. To me it's reminiscent of the Wile E Coyote cartoons I watched at the drive-in movies as a child. The coyote had a wide assortment of ACME products that he was always certain would help him catch the Road Runner. Sales people love it when they get us believing they'll make our lives easier.

You get the idea by now. Revisit it until you are able to start pausing yourself before your emotions run away! Think before you decide! Ask yourself the hard questions that blind optimism would allow you to ignore. It works and the payoff is huge!

Take a look back now! You should see some real distance accumulating from your starting point. Things should be making sense. You should be starting to see there are millions of ways to see and interpret things. You should be seeing that you have a choice! Okay, let's turn forward again! More detail on the mountains ahead! Let's carry on!

The Death Spiral of Doom

It sounds horrible, doesn't it? I made it up to some extent, however, there is something important and very obvious about almost everything I'll share with you in this book. This is just one more antidote of the same flavor of many.

The more you let things get out of control, the harder and harder it gets to regain control. If you tell yourself it's going to get worse, it usually will. If you spend so much time and energy worrying about things getting worse then you will fail to do anything to make them better.

Problems get amplified when we let things spiral out of control. Mild frustrations and annoyances become worse when we already feel buried. We often refer to it as the last straw that broke the camel's back.

The Death Spiral is also more commonly known as the self-fulfilling prophecy. You propose that something bad will happen and, either knowingly or unconsciously, you follow the sequence of events either realized or unrealized until your worst fears become reality.

Maybe you have seen a movie depicting a jet that is plummeting from the sky and the pilot freaks out, never regains control and the plane smashes violently into the ground. You may have also seen a movie where the pilot finds his composure, regains his senses, steers himself out of the tailspin and back into steady flight and is able to pull up in time to live to tell the story.

Life is very much about your ability to call a time-out when you begin to sense a tailspin! This will often save you from needing to be a cool cat who defies death. Ask yourself questions more often and you'll find yourself in fewer tailspins and your life will feel so much better!

Remember these words: simplify, simplify, simplify! The easier you make your life, the easier it will be! Don't think yourself into oblivion! Focus your energy on the solution whenever you encounter a new problem!

Change

We make changes in our lives when we are ready to accept the consequences of those changes. In order to make these changes we must accept both the known and unknown consequences those changes will bring!

Change is the paintbrush of time and our life is the canvas upon which its strokes are cast!

Many people see difficult life events as disasters. What these events often end up being, however, are bridges leading us to someplace different. It is greatly up to us to define, shape and manage change. These bridges can lead to opportunities; for every door that closes another opens. Most people never look for the other door to open. Instead, they only see closing doors and begin to feel very claustrophobic and isolated. They wallow in self-pity and the only thing they end up embracing is failure.

It often is the way we choose to look at things that have the most impact on our lives.

If we don't look for the doors that open, then we live in fear. This fear often becomes a self-fulfilling prophecy due to the paranoia, nervousness and depression it causes. In turn, all of these things affect how others view us, how we perform and, often, how people treat us. In my line of work and as a manager I have seen it too many times; those who live in fear and fail to embrace change always end up worse off.

The reality of life is that when bad things happen we almost always enter into the cycle of change. We begin by feeling loss, then depression, followed by feelings of denial or anger and, eventually, (sometimes after a long time, sometimes more quickly) acceptance. After we accept the change the full cycle of adaptation comes to a close and we are able to move on.

Understanding this cycle and realizing that it is often a waste of time helps us move through the stages with greater speed and ease. Accepting that some things are inevitable and relinquishing control helps us to shorten and skip much of the hard aspects of the change cycle. We are then free to view these changes as opportunities. By seeing both the doors that open and the doors that close and by making the very most out of our circumstances we often end up better than we were when we began. Try thinking of it like this: for every door you see change closing, you should see two more that change is opening.

Everyone just wants their life to be normal. Unconsciously, we often crave what we perceive as and believe to be normal. Consider though, that normal may be just the lie you have painted for yourself and that normal is merely a mirage in a very hot desert of desperation.

Change usually means a departure from what we have come to understand and accept as normal. Again, it's all about perspective; if we were to welcome change instead of fear it we would not struggle with these issues.

We must be prepared for change. I initially feared it because I was afraid it would alter my life and cause me to lose all I had, including material objects and the emotional investment I spent building a material life. It was only after I accepted the possible losses that I was able to start making changes. I came to believe that these changes and their rewards would outweigh any losses I might experience. Hindsight, timing, luck, however you want to slice it, I enjoy the new life I am living; simplification is very addictive!

I have found that less is more. The more junk I clear out of my life, the lighter and more nimble I feel. Materialism can be an extremely heavy anchor; it will hold us in place until we either raise it or cut the cord!

As I was getting ready to go to sleep last night, my wife and I conversed about today's world and the significance collegiate grades might (or might not) hold in the future. This discussion caused me to think in general about the need to accept that the world has changed. We have to figure out when we need to adapt versus when we need to hold on to our traditional values in order to help our children move forward. I think much of the grief we experience in life is caused by not knowing when to let things go. When do we just let go and stop allowing certain meaningless things to bother us?

Fear of change can hold our lives in neutral or even slip us into reverse if we aren't careful. We should understand and embrace that change is just a normal part of life. Watch your own change cycle, embrace it and accelerate through it. You'll notice that often the only difference between bad change and good change is the way you react to it.

Change is an event horizon. Whether the outcome will be good or bad is largely dependent upon the way the person who finds themselves, either as a part of the event or managing their interaction with the event. Many times events are not as personal as we make them out to be. Changes are as much opportunities as they are misfortunes.

When you first enter the change cycle, try to look ahead for the good in it as quickly as you can. By finding and accepting this true goodness, you'll find that the rest of the cycle will pass much faster. The art of asking your self questions is a key skill which will aid you in accepting change, making decisions and living a happier life.

Sitting At The Dock
Mark Abraham
San Francisco 2007

As the sun fell beneath the horizon, the city began to glow. I sat on the dock of the bay, sipped in the cool salty air, looked around and absorbed the atmosphere of the wonderful evening. I wondered how it was that I got to see so many wonderful things in this world and how lucky I was!

What IF

So many of us find ourselves saying: "If I only had this, I could do or be that!" Many people have hundreds of "if I only hads" or " if I only coulds".

These "if onlys" eventually cause us grief as they foster the notion that one change in a person's life equates to perpetual happiness. It's the equivalent, to some degree, of putting all of one's eggs into one basket. Sometimes we even make these changes - I have myself a few times - only to discover that there is another "If I only had" waiting beyond.

A happy life is about balance and creating harmony in our emotional and physical world. Balance is achieved in our state of mind and in our ability to clearly see our physical condition (health), situation, and environment.

By seeking balance in all these areas it's easier to find happiness. Complete happiness isn't guaranteed, however, and so perhaps on a scale of 1-100 we should think in terms of 51% being good, 65% being great and 75% being awesome. As I have said before, you can't know happiness without all of its counterparts to provide contrast. Life, by nature, is a struggle and sometimes it's very difficult. It's the contrast between difficulty and ease that make the good times mean something. If we were magically programmed at birth to accept and think it perfectly normal for our lives to be 80% bad, how different would the world and our lives look to us? It's kind of a bummer that we get conditioned to believe there should never be a bad or hard moment, huh?

The ability to ask ourselves **What If I** rather than stating **If I Only** can make a huge difference. **If I Only** is very wishful in nature whereas **What If I** internalizes the questions that help us to rationalize and plan changes based on our current situation, condition and environment. We should seek to ask ourselves **What If I** more often and then, over time, consider how to make the changes and what those changes would actually look like.

In terms of relationships, I believe if we ask ourselves a few questions we can gain a lot of clarity. Consider the following question. If I dated this person, what would our relationship look like in one year, three years, seven years, and beyond? If we see ourselves wanting to change our partners and make them into people they aren't, surely we are traveling on a dangerous and slippery slope by building expectations of them into which they have no input and probably no desire or ability to achieve.

One of the things I enjoy most about my current relationship is that we do not seek to change each other; we were very real and upfront about whom we were when we met and dated. My wife is truly my soul mate and best friend; she is perfect for me just the way she is.

Another thing worth mentioning about relationships is that when we hide our true feelings, wants and desires from our partners we deceive both them and ourselves. We are much better off when we keep it real! Sooner or later we just want to be ourselves and they just want to be themselves. When we pretend to be people we aren't and enter into long-term relationships, it's a recipe for disaster.

Finally, let's consider the notion of time in our modern world. I believe time is moving faster than most people can manage or deal with adequately. It's because modern times make communication and life so fast. We can jet to faraway places without seeing what lies between here and there.

We can passively text and communicate and also receive instant gratification or unhappiness. Technology has enslaved us in many ways; we work for it rather than allowing it to work for us. It's a grand mousetrap. It's only once we slow down and remove ourselves from its stealthy clutches that we realize the benefits of a slower pace. Slowing down allows us to take time to think, reflect, process our emotions, ponder our responses and interactions with others more carefully and, ultimately, to see the light. It's hard to be real and know what's authentic when we no longer deal with each other face to face.

I have seen people believe they are having relationships based on text messaging or online social networking. Without getting into the details, I believe this form of communication is extremely dangerous. People, in their text messages, are often not like or understood as their real selves. This makes sense. People want to be funny and witty in text and online mediums and the absence of body language and facial expressions makes exaggeration, deception and misunderstanding very common. I could, and someday may, write a whole book on social networking and the direction it's heading, however, I'll spare you and save that one for another day.

Sure, spontaneity is great, but I don't believe we are yet capable of living continuously spontaneous high speed lives; the velocity at which we sometimes travel is reckless in nature. This leaves us worn out if we don't take time to slow down, we are then less capable when life's real speed bumps occur, less able to muster the energy to deal with our real problems because all the unreal ones have sapped us dry.

My advice is to slow down, ask **What Ifs**, seek balance and look for more harmony in our lives.

No single event defines our destiny or our existence; it is the sum of what we make of our lives that is life itself, which gives us purpose, drives us forward and gives life meaning.

If we embrace this concept then we can face change and life with greater confidence and happiness.

Geyser Bison
Mark Abraham
Yellowstone National Park 2006

One magical afternoon when the bison came to play in a place where most would never dare to venture, my camera clicked.

We venture little and expect so much! Sometimes we imprison ourselves from within our mind and its limitations.

Parenting

Observing children has made me realize that so much of ourself is shaped during the process of growing up. Without having others in our lives, like both a mom and a dad, we cannot see the things that make those relationships work. This void plays a huge role in how we respond in the future.

Sometimes we miss out on the good programming because it's not available to us. Even witnessing an unsuccessful relationship between our parents builds a basis from which we'll make decisions in the future. When we observe we learn, formulate and then instate programming within ourselves.

While I'll probably never be qualified to write a book on parenting, I am compelled to share just a few thoughts on the subject.

A Mind for Life

My parents divorced while I was young and it had a profound impact on my life. I am not seeking pity or blaming my parents - this is not about that. In fact, elsewhere in this book you'll see that I find utility in the bad things that happen in life. As far as I can tell these experiences have made me, in the end, a better person. Perhaps this book would not exist if not for the way my life unfolded.

This chapter is about self-awareness with regards to parenting and the impact we have on our children's lives. Since I have been blessed to inherit children later in my life my thoughts may seem very evident to you. Rather than skipping past this chapter, however, I ask you to consider looking at your relationship with your children from an outside perspective.

Having not spent much time with my own father and then becoming a step-dad at age 43 has been quite an amazing experience. I suddenly found myself with four young ladies in my life. I seem to have lot in common with my stepdaughters and I am a very sympathetic father-figure in their lives.

The whole experience has been a little like a rocket ride where you find yourself accelerating from zero to 100,000 MPH in the course of mere seconds. Having had a little time now to look back at the distancing landscape, the view of what was then and is now provides a great amount of perspective.

I people watch quite a bit and, with regards to parenting, you can only imagine how much I have begun to watch and consider the actions of other parents. In the past, I really didn't have this opportunity. Of course, I reflect a lot upon my own childhood and how I can use those experiences to become a better parent myself.

Parenting

Most parents try to do the best they can. I often feel, however, like my best is not enough and I am sure many of you feel the same way. I also carry with me programming from movies and books about perfect parent figures. Perhaps it's Ward and June Cleaver, or some other more modern version of them. Smile! The few things I have learned I believe are important and, even at the risk of seeming naïve, I'll share my insights in an effort to provide you with a different perspective of your own relationship with your children.

It really is the small things that make a difference. I work hard to be at the girl's school and athletic events. It may not always seem like they care, but their feelings become more evident when you miss an event or see another parent missing one. These are the times and moments you'll never get back. The more you miss, the more distance it can create. To know a child is to have been a part of their life!

One of the hardest things I have dealt with in my life is building love and maintaining discipline! It can be tricky to try and become a parent, build trust and love, and provide structure and discipline all at once. You see, we often forget that life can be like a rocket ride to our children as well. Just as I accelerated into parenthood at Mach 5, these four young ladies also had to quickly adjust to having a new person in their life.

I believe that much of what I've developed in A Mind For Life has helped me in my journey. In the beginning, I found myself expecting too much from the girls. I also believe that as a parent there is value in taking notes, engaging with our children and asking them lots of questions about how they see and feel about things.

It's all too easy to forget our own childhood experiences and build unrealistic expectations for our children. I ask myself numerous times if I have the right expectations for the girls; if I am being fair and realistic; and if I could be doing better. I know it can be very hard and I am far from perfect!

There are literally a million variables we must try to juggle simultaneously in order to balance the scales of parenthood. It takes a herculean effort to keep all the moving parts from spilling everywhere!

Recognizing the importance of your engagement is huge. Recognizing that you have to maintain both discipline and love is also tremendously important. It's too easy to always cave and it's too harsh not to give in sometimes.

I once learned in a psychology class that bringing children to the adult level requires asking a lot of questions to actuate their awareness of their own thoughts and actions. This is not only valuable with children, but it also often works when you have a conflict with another adult. Asking questions, placing yourself in their shoes and choosing your battles carefully are a few of the things I wanted to mention. I encourage you not to assume or take these things for granted.

When's the last time you sat down and spent real quality time finding out about all the things going on in your child's life as a friend - not just as a parent? If you're attempting to be spiritually balanced, taking the time to be a good parent will enrich you. If you're bound to materialistic happiness, you'll never feel like you have enough time.

Additionally, taking notes describing your goals, core principles and values as a parent is also hugely important. If you revisit your list regularly, you can reprogram and become more like the parent you want to be.

Also, be sure to take a break and a little time off for yourself. In my opinion, you cannot be effective if you never recharge yourself. I talk about the importance of recharging elsewhere in this book. As you consider this notion, think about how being drained effects your ability to be a great parent!

In today's world, it's easy to forget that making your children work a little bit for the things they want will teach them to live better once they become independent. I call today's generation the Entitlement Generation. As you can see, the current economy is making gratuitous giving a more difficult feat for parents. Don't be afraid to make your children sweat a little for the things they want. They may, and likely will, find themselves in a world where it becomes increasingly difficult to buy material things. A spiritual life is far easier to achieve and leads to greater overall happiness.

Finally, making sure your expectations are realistic and focused on your children, not you, is a huge component to achieving balance. Just because they aren't aligning themselves to your dreams of them becoming important, powerful people doesn't mean they are failing. It also doesn't mean that they won't become great people someday. Remembering all the falls and tumbles you had to go through in order to learn life's lessons is helpful. Instilling spiritual richness in your children is valuable to their future and not caving to their material needs is worthy of frequent consideration.

A Mind for Life

We are wise as parents from our life experiences. We desperately wish we could save our children the pain and agony of the lessons we have learned.

The reality is that many lessons are, regrettably, only learned through failure. Having the courage and wisdom to let your children fail sometimes is the gold plating from which parenting is made. It's about you being aware enough of your children's lives to know when to make that call and when not to intervene that can and will make the difference.

Know your children and seek to manage the distance that can grow between you; it's a delicate balancing act for sure! The gift of your time is far more valuable in building strong children than opening your wallet. Of course the kids won't always agree! Smile!

The Difference You Make!

All too often we feel powerless in this world. As I was driving into work this morning I realized that perhaps we have more power than we could possibly imagine. It's the power to love, guide and interact positively with our children, spouses and all the other people with whom we associate.

Our lives help shape other people's lives. The very way we behave, the words we say, and the emotions we let play out are all very powerful in the big picture called life.

I was mad at one of the girls this morning and had been for days. My own hopes and expectations caused this feeling, not any major failure on her part. I love her and yet the emotions I was experiencing were creating a wedge between us. I was struggling to find a way to tell her the things I needed to say in a meaningful way. When children are younger it can be challenging to find an impactful way to communicate in order to get them to understand the messages we want to deliver.

I wanted to get rid of the wedge and I knew that, as the adult, it was be up to me to find the answers. This insight, as it so often does, developed over a period of weeks during which I had a realization, captured it in brief notes and worked on it until it was resolved. This is a powerful way to solve the problems in our lives.

Let's get back to the story! In a nutshell, I sensed I needed to make changes. As it turned out, there was much more to the issue than meets the eye. I realized that my feelings, expectations and the distance between us was being significantly amplified by other feelings and frustrations I was experiencing.

Whether our personal feelings and disposition are imagined or real, just or unjust, they are, in fact, our reality. Our behavior can and will be influenced by our perceptions of life. As it turns out, I was out of balance at this particular time and needed to rebalance myself. In the end it was so simple, I just needed to call a timeout, do some things for myself and have some conversations with my dearest friend in life, my wife.

Once I did that, I felt immensely better! This allowed me to see issues in my life with greater clarity and more acutely address the problem I wanted to solve.

In the end, I positioned our girl to successfully meet my expectations by prompting her to take care of her chores. I then took the time to focus positive energy and feelings towards her, allowing us to re-bond. I let her know I was aware I had been tough, re-emphasized her role in our family, explained the balance between give and take and lined up some fun activities we could do together.

Sometimes I think a major part of parenting is about knowing when a child's problem is really a problem and whether that child is at a point in their life where that problem can be successfully addressed. We gain this awareness by asking questions. Sometimes we must accept that the problem simply can't be solved at this point in time.

I also have been taking time with everyone to refocus and recommit to being the best influence I can in their lives and to be complimentary rather than contradictory.

This is the power of A Mind For Life! One of my greatest hopes for this book is that it will help you learn that there is great power in being able to step outside of yourself and your problems, get them down on paper if needed, review them and hone in on the underlying cause of the issue.

Real awareness provides you with the opportunity to make a difference in others' lives as well. If you can tune into them, craft and deliver your messages in a meaningful and impacting way, you will make a difference!

Once you have this awareness, you can work on a step-by-step solution that not only resolves the problem in the short-term, but also builds towards solving it for the long-term.

A Mind for Life

As for the girl in this story, not a lot changed on her part, it was change on my part that was needed!

Well, well! We have been marching awhile now. You've had your heads down for quite a bit. Look back and you can see you're making real progress!

Amused In The Mist

Mark Abraham
Yellowstone National Park 2006

The mist like a veil of mystery over pools of time! We follow the line like good little people, seemingly impervious to the veil of fog that hangs over us. We can see clearly again when we step out of the patterns everyone follows and think for ourselves!

Mirror, Mirror

I found it difficult to decide where in this book to discuss the following subject. I believe most people will find the concept easy to understand but the task itself to be very difficult.

A Mind For Life is all about awareness, often focusing on cultivating a stronger awareness of people's natures and the dynamics of the lives we lead. The hardest task to master, however, is self-awareness.

I am not sure if the inability to accurately see ourselves is a result of external programming. Instead, I believe it's built into human psychology; it is fundamentally essential to survival and life. Because of this, it's a difficult subject for many of us to explore.

If, for example, you saw me as a mystic or super human who could tell you what is causing and will continue to cause you to fail in your life and I walked up to you and asked; "Do you want to know what is holding you back in life?" you would most likely answer: "Yes."

I think most of us want to know what is keeping us from success. Up to this point, it sounds easy enough.

If I told you it was your own fault and proceeded to give you a list of all of your faults which contributed to your failure we would likely enter into a very tense conversation. Most people's reaction to such analysis is to be defensive. Most people deny that they have faults.

Let's dive right and discuss some key concepts. The perception others have of you will become your reality. Like it or not, if you are seen a certain way, whether it's anchored in truth or based on some false notion, you are and will be treated in accordance with their views. I frame it this way because easing you towards recognizing your faults is a lot more effective than simply tossing you in the pool to either sink or swim.

So, in part, I am offering you an out - you may not really be as people see you; however, if you want to get ahead, you need to change their perception. Changing people's perceptions is a very difficult business. It often becomes argumentative in nature and arguments, all too often, are ineffective in changing someone's mind.

Then how can you succeed in managing perception?

What I have learned is that it's much easier to generate new perceptions than it is to change old perceptions. Generate enough

Mirror, Mirror

positive new perceptions about yourself and people will later question whether their old perceptions were accurate.

Worst case scenario: they will believe you have changed and be more willing to work with the new you.

Although this method is a great secret, it is relatively easy to generate new perceptions. Just remember, the more bad perceptions you created the more good new perceptions it will take to change people's minds. You must do more than simply create new perceptions – it is essential that you maintain them as well. If the flaws you actually possess lead you back down a path that generates negative perceptions, you'll soon find yourself back in the same place you started. Therefore, we must return to the beginning in order to really tackle the larger issues.

The real secret, as I stated earlier, is easy to understand, but very difficult for most to master. Simply stated, you have to be able to recognize and manage your real faults. For many of us, our psychological make-up makes it difficult to identify our own faults. Conversely, those of us with low self-esteem see our faults too easily, creating a whole different set of problems.

The first thing to do when delving into your own faults is to take a deep breath and realize that you must remain calm and open. It helps to tell yourself, up front, that you aren't going to react until you have taken inventory and considered all of your faults. Furthermore, keep in mind that you are usually hugely rewarded once you effectively complete this exercise.

You might start by developing a list of your faults as follows:

I am impatient
I am selfish
I am not very sensitive to others needs
I do not listen very well
I am grumpy all the time
I am too impulsive
I am unhealthy because of my diet

Of course the list will likely become quite lengthy. If it doesn't then you probably aren't being honest with yourself. If you struggle, seek external feedback.

I'll warn you now: to be successful you must create a very open and friendly environment for others to share their feedback with you. After they share you should show gratitude rather than hostility and anger. Remember, they are doing you a huge favor by sharing their perceptions. In essence, they are handing you the treasure of future success. Arguing with them will do little to change their perception. In fact, it may even strengthen it.

It's very important that you don't let the feedback you receive from others create distance between you. If they're being honest with you, their assertions may hurt quite a bit. This feedback could cause you to experience a lot of negative emotions, including disdain towards those people who have shared their thoughts with you.

I don't really recommend asking someone you love and need in your life for input. Again, keep the big picture in mind; they are helping you! You must also realize that some people may refuse to provide you with feedback simply because they fear your reaction or they feel what they have to say is simply too hurtful.

Sometimes, they believe their feedback will do little to affect or change you.

With this in mind, there are several other ways you can find out more about yourself. Personality tests are one source, and, believe it or not, professional astrology can sometimes be another. I remember as a kid my mom was always telling me how I was cranky and moody because my sun sign was Cancer and that I was impatient because I had an Aries moon. I must confess - I am moody and impatient - so I have to laugh about it! Self-acknowledgement has done me a world of good. It's not the astrology itself that's really relevant; it's simply a source of feedback with which you can compare yourself. It's that comparison to the analysis that is important. Self-assessments, life coaches, siblings and your parents are also decent sources of input.

It takes an extraordinary human being to be able deal with your own faults. If you master this you truly will exist on a higher plain. While it may sound negative, there is tremendous comfort and peace in being able to understand your faults. It gets even better when you can start dealing with them.

It helps to choose a few problem areas (the most important) and work on them rather than attempting the whole list at once. Identify the faults you believe cause you the most grief.

It also helps to propose a positive statement of how you want to be in order to modify your behavior. Let's take one fault, explode it, and formulate the positive modification to our behavior.

Fault:
I don't listen well.

Reason:
I am self-centered and impatient. As a result, I always feel rushed to move forward. This causes me to skim over what people say while I'm attempting to listen to them. I also try to multitask when listening to other people.

What it's costing me:
People stop talking to me and I miss out on a lot of important things that impact my career and relationships. When you listen to others you gain their respect and trust. My failure to listen has led me to make stupid mistakes in my career and created a lot of distance in my relationships. Because I don't listen, I don't even know the full extent of what the cost is of having this problem.

What I will do differently:
I will make sure I have time to listen to others. I will take notes. If I am too busy at that time to listen, I'll let that person know and schedule time with them when I can sit, focus and listen. I'll make sure I don't put it off for too long, therefore, the person needing to be heard will understand that I care. I will make sure there are no distractions. I will tell myself it's important to listen. I will ask questions about what the person is telling me. I'll make sure I understood what the person told me. I'll actually consider what it is they are communicating to me. I'll make sure they know that I understand and acknowledge what they have said. If what they said requires action on my part I will develop a plan and get agreement with that person on what I will or will not do. I'll make sure to give myself credit for listening!

Ok, so now that we have exploded a single fault, let's dig a little more into the process.

The "what I will do differently" realm contains several important elements. Personally, it has often been a challenge for me to remember people's names. A trick someone taught me is to make sure you note a person's name when they are giving it. You can do this by saying the person's name silently three times, "Your name is Jane Doe, your name is Jane Doe, your name is Jane Doe." You then ask yourself, "Who is she?" and answer "Jane Doe." Although I didn't realize it until recently, this process allows us to program ourselves to remember someone's name.

We need to do these types of things when we are attempting to modify our behavior. The key elements to reprogramming at this level are to become self-aware, execute the what you will do differently portion of the new program, including asking questions in the exercise and providing yourself positive enforcement or a mini reward as a way of acknowledging successful execution of the new programming.

By focusing on a few faults each week and looking at the overall list every time in order to assess your progress, you will make major leaps in improving upon your faults.

This all assumes, of course, that you want to change your faults. If you aren't committed to making the changes, it's probably pointless to try. I've found that people often say, "It's too hard! You know what? I've done pretty well being the way I am, so I don't think I really need to change."

It's truly up to you. You cannot know what you don't understand and don't try to learn. That's my only response to this sort of reasoning. You'll never know if fixing your faults can make a difference if you don't try to change and see what life is like on the other side.

I won't lie to you. This chapter is very difficult and can cause you a lot of heartache and grief in the short run. It will be easy to quit and remain as you are. This is why I have a cost factor included in assessing your faults. Look at the costs and determine if you can live with them. This will help you to decide whether you need to make a change or not.

Of course, if you change perception and fail to address the root cause of that perception, sooner or later the original perception will return and you'll be back to square zero. As a manager of people, I have seen this many times in others. As an individual, I have seen how the failure to address the true root cause of perceptions has impacted my own life.

I do realize this all sounds very cold and mechanical. Dealing with your faults, at first, is hardly a pleasant experience. Our inherent psychology deliberately blinds us to many of our faults. It's what keeps us wanting to live and moving forward. It's why we always look better in the mirror than we actually are. It's essential to have this self-esteem because much of our will to live comes from it.

In closing, be careful not to beat yourself to death. Balance is the key; that's why recognizing and improving your faults is so very rewarding. Remember to try fixing a few things at a time and not all of them at once!

After some work, you'll notice that the image you see in the mirror is finally real! Real is very refreshing, energizing and will lead to a lot of happiness.

Pearls Of Wisdom

Write down what you learn in life, take life notes!

Life notes, you ask? Do you think I'm joking or simply insane? Seriously, even though you're no longer a student, those note-taking skills you learned in school can help you a lot in life. This book, for instance, is a result of my own life notes. I wrote down the things I learned and formed them into desirable new behaviors and character traits.

It might have been my nature or just dumb luck that drove me to write down and analyze my reflections on major life lessons. I even compiled these lessons into a list entitled Life Meanings, which you'll find near the end of this book. That list was my attempt at capturing lessons I learned throughout my life; much of what I share in this book is derived from those very first notes. The more I referred to and acted upon these notes, the more confidence

I gained in my behavioral modifications and responses to life events.

As you read the list you'll probably think I sure had a lot of lessons to learn. I'd contend that we all do. Often we don't realize the lessons we have learned. Without this realization, we fail to modify our behavior and end up learning the same lessons over and over. Interestingly, because we traverse many emotions during every life event, we are able to harvest many lessons from a single incident. What I've done in this book is developed a framework for managing these emotions. In my opinion, that education can then be reapplied to our daily lives and assist us as we navigate through future events.

This framework, however, is not perfect! Life Meanings changed several times over a ten-year period. Sometimes I had to make wholesale changes concerning how we should manage our emotions; other times the changes were more in the spirit of fine-tuning.

Whether you elect to directly adopt what I've accumulated in my collection or build your own personalized framework, the technique of capturing your profound and deep thoughts in the form of notes will almost certainly benefit you. You can swizzle the framework around in your mind, explore possibilities, experiment and cultivate these notes into life changing beliefs, behaviors and philosophies.

Capturing meaningful thoughts can be a bit of a chore. It requires you to be aware of your thought process, to be able to capture the essence of each thought, and then, later, to explore and refine your thoughts in order to completely distill them. The discipline it requires can be annoying. Many times I've had to roll myself out of bed after I was settled in order to capture a thought. It's also a challenge to capture them while you are driving, showering, working or in the middle of a meeting. To this day I still lose many thoughts simply due to the logistics of life.

These days I often use my phone to take a note and refer back to it later. I've learned to capture the essence of my thoughts in one or two quick sentences. Later, when I have more time, I return and expand the thoughts in greater detail. The trick is to expand on each thought while it's still fresh in your mind.

Did you know that this chapter, in fact, began as a note? My original note is the first line; I deliberately left it intact in order to illustrate my point.   Below are two more examples of brief notes that I plan to expand on soon; all three were captured in a single entry in my phone.

"Chasing dreams and how they change when you get older and how you're not really giving up on your dreams"

"Reconciling what you want and what is compatible with your life is perhaps one of the most difficult things to do."

Look for these thoughts later in the book; I'll speak to them in due time. When you are making these notes, don't worry about grammar. Instead, aim to capture substance when you jot down your thoughts. Make sure you give yourself enough material so you are able to expand upon your original note.

Human beings are the most magnificent machines on earth! Think of us in that spirit: mixtures of minds and bodies. These combined qualities, through our inspiration and labor, have allowed us to create all material things. You too can and will be profound if you are able to capture your own thoughts. Remember, even if it's profound to you and only you, it's still profound!

How do you know when you're having a thought worth capturing? Sometimes you feel it, like an electric surge, and you know you're having a profound moment. Other times this recognition requires more work.

I sometimes liken it to conscious dreaming! I learned long ago, as a child, how to control my dreams. I read a book on astral projection and my young mind was swept away by the notion that through dream control I could experience anything I wanted. While I didn't really achieve that level of control, I was able to become aware while I was dreaming - particularly during bad dreams. I knew that I was merely dreaming and was able to wake myself up, cause my dreaming self to laugh, or redirect myself to a better, easier dream. That's right; awareness can even be obtained within a dream. You can take that awful nightmare of falling off a cliff and turn it into a risk-free bungee jump. Turn a fearful experience into something fun!

I find it much easier to trigger awareness when I reach a troubled moment in a dream. If a dream is easy and free there is no need for me to abort or control the experience. There must be something extraordinary happening in order to trigger my consciousness.

It's this same way when we attempt to capture our profound thoughts. If we train ourselves to recognize these thoughts it becomes easy to capture them. The first key is to realize when you are feeling intense emotion. Creating a daily reminder to look for these intense moments is how we begin to actually recognize them. This is one of the key general techniques in reprogramming. Yes, even recognizing our own profound thoughts requires reprogramming, just like controlling our dreams.

The human brain is fabulous and since we lack the ability to fully access its immensity, it's largely untapped. I imagine that reprogramming experiments could potentially reveal many capabilities of which we are currently unaware.

Try a daily reminder to look for profound thoughts and then start capturing them. Also, you may consider capturing notes on positive and negative emotions. I'll talk about The Path at the end of this book but, for now, when you experience intense positive emotions simply capture a thought on them and go back and revisit your note later.

Once you capture thoughts, ideas and emotions the next step is to revisit these notes and twirl them around in your mind. I ask myself many questions in order to stimulate my creative thought process.

Why did this generate the emotions it did?
What if I responded differently?
Do I like the way I was impacted or responded?
Is there a better way?
Is it natural to feel this way and why?
Do all people feel this way?
Why do we respond or get impacted this way?
In three days from now, in a week or a month, how will I feel about this?

Is the response a result of programming and what type of program?

How would I write this as a future pearl of wisdom for change or reinforcement that I can read over and over again each month?

These questions should provide you with a jumping off point as you begin to explore your own thoughts!

The last step in this process is to revisit the pearls of wisdom you create over and over again. You can even arrange them in order of the frequency you feel you need to revisit them. As you begin to master certain concepts you can revisit them less frequently, devoting more time to the ideas you have yet to master.

You'll find the more you visit a pearl the easier and faster it is to reprogram yourself. This speed is limited, however, by how entrenched a program is. Some programs are very deeply rooted, perhaps even genetically encoded into you, and they can be extremely difficult nuts to crack. With work, however, you can begin to control these programs, even if they are never fully disposed of!

Remember to craft your pearls as positive behaviors. For example, "I'll seek to listen more carefully as it will lead to me to be more enlightened and create more rewards in my life."

Another thing to keep in mind is that you can break problems apart. For example, you may be programmed to be angry whenever you see a certain person from your past. You may never be able to stop that initial flood of emotion but you might be able to alter the way you allow that emotion to impact your day.

I've elected not to withhold any secrets in this book! Therefore, you could take the framework I have presented in this chapter and literally reinvent your life. Much of what is presented in the rest of this book builds upon and reinforces this premise. Think of this as the basement or foundation. We still need to build the house.

It's my hope that after reading this book, capturing your own notes and learning to use the tools I am offering that you will be moving towards making the changes you want in your life. It should allow you to craft a plan that is tailored to your specific needs and priorities.

Complimentary Existence

If there is a Yin and a Yang to my book, this is it! Much of our lives are spent running against the current instead of with it. Life can seem like we are swimming upstream and, to some degree, we often are.

I got to thinking about this concept while reading one night. While I won't get into specifics about the material, it was about parenting and it led me to realize that I hadn't been being as complimentary to one of our girls as I could've been.

She has a creative imagination and explores ideas in her mind. I was always being the voice of reason: explaining the flaws in her ideas and why they wouldn't work. In retrospect, my behavior seems really harsh. At the moment, I felt like I had been grounding her in reality. In hindsight, however, I feel that perhaps I was just stifling her creativity.

Upon realizing this I really changed the way I approached our girl's ideas. I've been reprogramming myself to be positive and encouraging and mixing my wisdom into the conversation by asking questions that safely and creatively stimulate her to think and explore her ideas more deeply. I still fail sometimes; reprogramming takes time and, in parenting, it takes extra effort!

While this example is limited and simplistic it does introduce the concept pretty well. To take it further we must look at all of our relationships and interactions with others. When you feel frustrated and stressed you should come back to this concept and consider what might be causing you to feel the way you do. As your self-awareness grows, your ability to stop your emotions mid-flight will get better and better. By doing this you'll be able to help yourself avoid a lot of stress and also prevent a lot of poor reactions to other people and situations.

I use this same strategy in my work. I try to realistically assess my employees' abilities and talents and map my expectations and their roles in ways that complement their abilities and help them to grow. Doing this makes everyone involved more successful. I also don't assume I have nothing new to learn. In fact, more days than not, I learn from others and grow myself.

I invest more energy in seeing other people's perspectives than I do in conveying my own. I also try, in my mind, to walk in their shoes for awhile. While this doesn't usually change my views or cause me to agree with them, it does greatly help me understand where they are coming from and why they feel the way they do. To be successful in influencing other people it's critical to understand what motivates and drives them. The chapter on communicating will also introduce the concept that it is your own responsibility to make others understand your perspective.

When you are confronted with someone whose viewpoints oppose your own, it is important to attempt to find a common and higher ground that you both agree on. If you then map your efforts towards this end, wonderful things will begin to happen. As you come together, your lower level disagreements will begin to lose their weight and no longer push you away from each other.

I confess that there is one problem with everything I'm trying to convey to you! While what I'm teaching you can bring much peace to your life, it can also create new challenges! Perhaps the easiest and most direct way to convey this is to say that if you spiritually or mentally move to a higher plain, you may feel isolated if you are traveling alone. You will have to accept that even though you're changing, others may not be. Influence will help you remain harmonious with them and the lure of the higher purpose or meaning you bring to your needs will bring them along with you.

In terms of programming, this is what I call fatal loop. Bettering ourselves and simply expecting others to also be better is a problematic expectation. If you want others to walk the path of self-improvement you must accept the responsibility of showing them the way.

The answer to this problem is, for me, to simplify and focus on the love I have for those closest to me. Accept and embrace them, enjoy their presence in your life and feel the peace and comfort they provide. If they are your children or other loved ones, perhaps you can share what you've learned. The key is to have no expectations - don't let their failure to learn or embrace the lessons you provide become the source of your discontentment.

Let's discuss a few more related items before we wrap up this chapter.

Individuality is a complex notion that can cause a lot of disruption in our Yin Yang discussion. When to exert your individuality and when to repress it is often a difficult decision. If it is not accepted, exerting your individuality may come at a high price. People may label you weird or stupid or hurl other insults at you when you don't conform to their view of how people should be.

Some people are taught that asserting your individuality is a sure path to rapid failure. Others, however, teach that you shouldn't be afraid to be yourself; they encourage you to always assert your individuality and pay no attention to the opinions of others. No wonder this is all so confusing!

Let's revisit a concept I discussed earlier in this book. Perception is reality. How we are perceived by others definitely has an impact on us. Ultimately, I can't tell you how to choose. You'll have to decide if your individuality and others' perception of it allows you to achieve your desired results. I assert my individuality when it's important to me and the people with whom I'm interacting.

For example, the man on the street corner, who I don't know and never will, has no need to know what my political beliefs are. We must choose our battles wisely. In order to do so, we must also consider when our individuality will put us at odds with others and/or generate negative perception that will impact us in meaningful ways.

Complimentary Existence

Individuality is made up of many components. This complex network includes your personality and general demeanor as well as your self-esteem, your treatment of others and all of your emotional postures. We can easily find ourselves disliked and lonely if we are not mindful of the perception we create.

Sometimes who we are and believe we need to be at work is very different from the authentic self we share with our friends and families.

I guess my point is really relatively simple. Awareness of your individuality and the way it impacts your life is relevant to the grand scheme of achieving self-awareness and developing A Mind For Life.

In my mind, harmony is akin to emotional nirvana. Seek the path of harmony with others, seek the higher ground and seek to simplify your life and you will, inevitably, feel more at peace and experience greater happiness.

The cost of your individuality may be more expensive than you ever imagined. Most highly individualistic people fail to see how their uniqueness sometimes leads to feelings and perceptions of elitism and causes them to feel lonely and isolated.

This requires a great deal of self-awareness and intense thought about whether we want to pay the price associated with our individuality. Once again, I employ the method of asking questions.

What prices do I or will I pay?
Why is it important to me?

Does it make my life more complicated?
Is it worth it?

The funny thing about human nature and willpower is that despite logically answering these questions in a way that points towards abandoning our individuality due to its high cost, many people assert it anyway. Why is that?

Often we justify this assertion by expecting that everyone should simply accept us for who we really are. While that is a very noble notion to consider, the reality is that people don't always accept our individuality. In addition, we often project our expectation of acceptance onto others without holding ourselves to the same standard.

I began this chapter discussing how we can become complementary with others. Seeking the higher and nobler ground that sits above both us and others will almost always be a more rewarding way to approach our differences. When we balance our own needs along with the needs of others we are able to find the common higher good. Once we find this common ground, we stop caring so much about expressing our own individuality. Our focus shifts to the oneness we can find with others and with life itself.

Tinker Creek

Mark Abraham
Cleveland, Ohio 2008

Sometimes there is no explanation for the simple freedoms we find in nature. Walking in a creek barefoot on a hot summers day, exploring and chatting away an afternoon.

Mind, Body And Soul

Sometimes we have to delve into the shadows in order to give our eyes a break from the brightness. This chapter is very diverse and will encompass some strange ideas. At times, it will border on the abstract.

You may have been exposed to the concept that the truth is sometimes only derived by exposing everything that is false.

I, like others before me, propose that often by exploring the unknown, the seemingly absurd, and the abstract we can open our minds to seeing things differently and achieve a higher plane of thought.

To experience diversity is to grow your awareness!

A Mind for Life

If we are never exposed to darkness, we cannot understand the significance of light. We can't truly appreciate color if we aren't exposed to black and white.

Even though I mention them at times, whether you believe in things such as science or religion is irrelevant to our discussion. You don't have to adopt my personal beliefs. Instead, you must form your own beliefs and be personally accountable to them. Looking outside your normal purview, however, may help as you are attempting to define your own personal beliefs.

When I was young, I remember getting a book from the library on Astral Projection. I am not even sure how I became aware of the subject, but I was as fascinated with it as most young boys are with the X-ray glasses they see advertised in the back of comic books.

I think what attracted me to the idea of astral projection was the thought of being able to travel, fly and possess superhuman powers without ever having to step foot out of my house. I couldn't even tell you today how it works because I read the book so many years ago. I mention it here because it introduces the idea of separation of body and mind; the body can sometimes be thought of as simply an extension of or vessel for the mind. I am speaking loosely and symbolically here, so don't think too deep on it!

Religion introduces us to the notion that we have a spirit or soul and that it is, in essence, independent of our mind and body and extends beyond the limits of time as we know it. Some religions propose the idea of an afterlife or a judgment day beyond the physical limitations of death and our human bodies. For the most part, people base their beliefs on their spirituality; they have life-long relationships with their God and values.

Only a few hundred years ago, scientists had to convince the masses that the world wasn't flat. At the time, most people absolutely accepted the notion that the world was flat. Even though it was seen as truth at that time, in hindsight, the idea was completely false.

I could go on like this for hours; however, it's time to try to connect these ideas to my main point. What we know and accept as fact today is, in reality, subject to change over time. Many of us base our beliefs off of ideas we believe to be factual even though others see them as rooted in faith. Today's truth may be exposed as something far less concrete in the future. History has tremendous value in proving this concept, we only need to study it in order to witness how what we view as fact has changed over time. Our beliefs, nonetheless, are in fact our truths and we live our lives accordingly.

Awareness in my opinion shouldn't be limited to what we know and believe today. Any great advances have transcended the status quo and past beliefs, and shifted the paradigm toward a new way of understanding and seeing things.

By loosening up a little and allowing ourselves to explore other thought processes and beliefs we are able to expand our own awareness. By exploring ideas which many people believe to be false, we either confirm or expand our own beliefs.

My point is that we shouldn't limit ourselves. It is important to step outside the box, to consider new ways of thinking and to imagine, for a few moments, that the X-ray glasses are real. Your awareness, understanding and compassion for others will greatly be enhanced. Ask questions rather than making convictions upon a set of fixed beliefs.

By embracing the possibility that things may be different than we originally thought and by working to understand the beliefs of others we will find greater harmony and with greater harmony comes greater peace and happiness. You can't metaphorically walk in another person's shoes if you have no understanding of what it's like to actually wear them.

Regardless of your beliefs about how the Mind, the Body and the Soul truly exist, harmony will create a more positive environment and a greater sense of oneness with everything and everyone.

Once we achieve this oneness then the separation of mind, body and soul becomes irrelevant - during those moments we simply are.

Look at all of your material possessions (especially the big ones) and assess their true value in your life. How important is your miracle blender, your super fancy car or your dream home to your life?

Inevitably, many of these possessions will have lost their meaning to you. While you are looking at all the things you had to have in order to make your life better and realizing that they really represent clutter or boat anchors ask yourself this: Would you still acquire them again? With this insight, how do you propose to live, going forward, in relation to material things?

Mind, Body And Soul

Mental Aspirations - Taking a mental inventory of your wants and needs can be tremendously valuable. Wanting to be famous, rich, smart, strong, fit, etc. - what does it all mean, what's its value, what's its place and how much of it should you attempt to control?

Spirituality doesn't have to be a material-free nirvana where we live with little or nothing and walk around looking and feeling like we are always high.

That is not be the goal of AM4L. There are plenty of cults a person can find and subscribe to if they are looking for such a short-term, delusional way of life.

Life, in my opinion, is about obtaining a balance between reality and the programming we live with and finding a bigger piece of the happiness pie that will sustain us for the long run!

Getting everything we want is simply not good for us. Often, it leads to a greater level of dissatisfaction and a disconnection from what I call oneness. Usually, when we get what we want, it's not everything we imagined - the reality simply can't match the fantasy we created in our minds.

This same concept applies to other aspects of our lives, including love and relationships. We create fantastic expectations that, in reality, are unattainable.

Sometimes we believe we have found peace and happiness only to emerge from our disillusion and face the cold hard reality that we were totally fooling ourselves. In relationships, this often occurs when we find an irresistibly good looking person. We want a relationship with them so badly that we project all kinds of qualities upon them. We buy into this fantasy and believe we have found our soul mate only to crash into reality like a train hitting a wall at a hundred miles per hour.

How, then, are we supposed to deal with our wants and desires on a spiritual level? Many religions teach us that these things are bad, and in some cases, they are. Remember, not everything we want is good for us. But, without want and desire, what do we live for? Without them, where does our drive come from?

This is why balancing reality is so important. There are certain basic human needs, among them: food, water, shelter, security and love. Some of us choose to fulfill these needs to higher levels than others. For some of us a shack will do while others feel they need nothing less than a mansion. Some of us want exotic foods while others simply want enough food and drink to maintain their existence.

In today's world we are expected to meet a certain level of needs. The average American, for instance, is expected to have an apartment, a small family and enough food to get by each month. In order to maintain these things they must also have a job.

So if you have these basics, then what? Can that be enough for you? For some of us it is, for others it is not. It depends on how hard earning the money seems, how good and fulfilling the relationships and family are and how safe and secure everyone feels. Ironically, in a family environment, one person may have all they need and be happy while another person may feel deprived and unhappy. That unhappiness impacts others and drives them to feel and act a certain way. Yes, the capacity of others to be happy impacts your own happiness. For now, however, we will ignore that fact.

The amount of time we spend on maintaining our basic needs obviously impacts the amount of time we spend enjoying ourselves. In addition, much of what we are programmed to like and enjoy in life is influenced by hyper-advertising, peer pressure and spin. Like it or not, it's difficult to simply give up these ideals. A rotten apple may not be made fresh again.

How others treat us and how they interact with us plays a huge role in maintaining balance. People can create problems for us or we can find happiness in simply chatting with friends.

Many of these things may seem fairly obvious and dull; so let's move forward!

A material path and belief in the material world often stems from our belief that God doesn't exist and can't do anything to fulfill our wants and needs. This is particularly true for people who desire a lot of material objects. Ironically, these people often blame God for their lack of material satisfaction. Those who attempt to and are unable to fill their hearts and souls with material objects often turn away from God, never realizing that He delivers spiritually, not materially.

The more spiritually satisfied we become the less we rely on material objects to bring us happiness. This is tied to the concept of simplicity I've previously spoken about. Happiness can be so simple to achieve when we approach it from a spiritual perspective.

A Mind for Life

God means different things to many people; I don't mean to be blasphemous. Some find God in nature, others in the night sky – some even think sitting at a ball game eating hotdogs is divine.

Despite my personal belief in God, I believe spirituality, in large part, is about oneness with life. I know I feel this oneness while I'm watching a sunset, driving down a highway and pondering life with my hand out the window carving out shapes in the wind and while existing in many other inexpensive immaterial ways.

The process of fulfilling our basic needs is not relevant to our discussion; it's accepted. I find that keeping my needs as simple as possible makes my life easier and allows me to be less connected to the material aspects of life and more frequently connected with the free side of existence. It is through this simplicity that we are able to feel more spiritual, more at one with the world and more connected to our beliefs about God and ourselves.

Again, I am not suggesting that you should start wearing a robe, smoking pot and living on a mountain! I am simply saying that the more you get in touch with simple pleasures and reduce your material dependence, especially if you're not rich, the more likely you are to find it easier to cover your basic needs.

This leads to being able to enjoy the simplicity of thought and relationships and becoming more connected with life, nature, others, your spiritual beliefs and, of course, yourself! Once you sort through all this and go back to taking your inventory, you may find that much of what you originally thought was important in life is now meaningless.

Mind, Body And Soul

This is why so many rich people look and sound like they are half dead when you view and talk to them. Often they are materially, not spiritually, rich. Think about this within the context of your own life and consider whether you might want to make changes.

Reflections
Mark Abraham
Olathe, Kansas 2002

Life has many layers in which we can get lost and it becomes difficult to discern the sky from the rocks in the river. When we relax our focus for a bit we can separate them and life becomes clear.

Needs, Needs, Needs

It's helpful to sit down and reflect on the balance between where we actually are in our lives and where we want to be.

From time to time I have used this technique with friends and it's been very helpful. Try to view this as a framework for analyzing your needs and wants. In order to gear the framework to your personal situation, you may expand and modify it as needed.

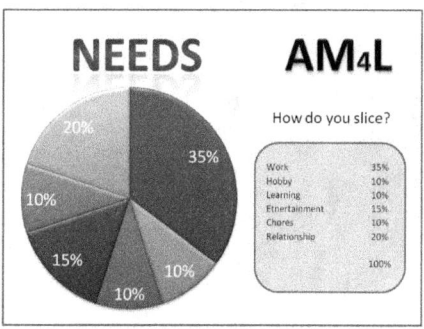

A Mind for Life

The crude graph above represents a person's desired needs. The thought is that each of us should develop a pie chart showing how much focus we would like to devote to each portion of our life. You can just grab some scrap paper and a pencil and make your own chart - nothing fancy is needed, just your time and mind.

Of course many people don't want to work, but the idea is to represent your life in a reasonable way. If 40 hours a week is the norm for a job and there are a total of 112 waking hours a week (assuming we sleep 8 hours each night) then work should represent a little more than one-third of a working person's waking hours (including preparation for and travel to and from the office).

It's natural for us to want to devote time to our relationships, perhaps time to watch TV or go to movies, time to enjoy our hobbies and time to take care of personal business such as paying bills, laundry, etc.

The idea is to reasonably illustrate the balance we hope to achieve in the amount of time we devote to a given set of activities in our lives, at a high level.

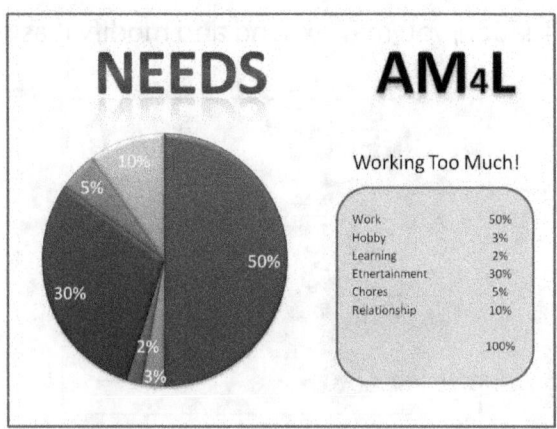

Needs, Needs, Needs

Our next mission then is to create a chart based on the way we are currently living our lives. In the example above we see that, in reality, this person is working during half of their waking hours and that the time they devote to their relationships and personal responsibilities is greatly diminished.

This should sound an alarm! It's not healthy to maintain this state for extended periods of time. You may note that the focus on entertainment actually increased; this is typical for someone that works too much. They have a tendency to want to escape as compensation for their increased work efforts.

It gets difficult to respond to an analysis like this for a person who finds this to be their real life situation. They often feel their job requires or even demands this much time. I can tell you that if this person is married, this is a very classic example where the marriage will begin to deteriorate if left unattended. Their relationships with their children will also be affected.

When we fail to make corrections and take matters into our own hands, life has a funny way of turning over the control of our lives to someone else. If you don't tend to your marriage then your spouse may decide you're not going to be married anymore. This is a classic example where a failure to react causes you to lose any control over a situation. Likewise, if you fail to pay the bills then bill collectors and attorneys will take over.

While those are extreme situations, maintaining balance is very important to your happiness. In the previous example, sooner or later the person will realize that keeping their job is their own choice. If you are in a similar situation and your job is creating imbalance in your life, you should, at the very least, look for another position.. Keep in mind that our perception of what we need to do to keep our job is often skewed by our fear of insecurity.

The fear of insecurity is influenced by many other life variables. For example, having a lot of debt can cause us to feel more paranoia concerning maintaining our jobs. When we start to look at the big picture of life and how society programs us to buy, buy again and then buy even more, it gets easy to envision some evil puppet master sitting above us pulling all the strings. I would contend, however, that it's more about our own ability to control our lives and keep things simple. If we believe someone else is pulling all the strings that can be a problem in itself.

Build your own pie charts and use them as you analyze the challenges you face in your life and consider the gap between the way your life is and the way you want it to be. I realize that this may be the Mr. Spock seemingly Vulcan approach to life, but it really does work. If you are already dismissing it, maybe you can add that to your list of faults! Smile!

It helps to revisit and revise your chart every few months in order to see how things are progressing. After awhile you'll be able to construct them in your head.

Dreams And Future

Living out small dreams has limited significance to who you are!

You can climb a mountain just like a famous person did and you will feel a sense of connectedness, pride and exhilaration. Some hours, days, weeks months later, however, YOU will be YOU again. Life will be as it was before and you'll be forced back to reality.

What was will become a memory, and its significance may eventually be born out in reflections of what has passed, and some may be or may have actually been a part of your core being already.

Because we spend so much time trying to live our lives the same way others do or expect us to instead of being ourselves and living our own lives, we often find ourselves facing the starkness of reality: feeling empty, confused and incomplete.

A Mind for Life

I realize these may seem like bleak words; not every idea or concept you'll capture will be exhilarating. Nevertheless, these notions are still significant and can help shape our direction.

Such is the case with these words! This may be a somewhat disturbing chapter. Even though this idea may be controversial in nature, it should stir you to reflect upon your own life and behaviors.

I remember the day I first recognized and captured part of this idea. I was out on a bike ride, something I was doing almost daily back then, and riding on my route and I passed a house where a gentleman was in his driveway working on his Harley.

Inside his garage was a neon Harley sign, a magnificent tool bench, beer advertising signs, a beer neon light and a group of friends standing just inside sipping on some frosty mugs of draft beer they had pulled from his in-house beer tap. They were dressed in biker gear and bandanas; they looked like stereotypical bikers.

It occurred to me that they were playing the part really well. I hate to be judgmental, but most of us are when we encounter people we perceive as different from ourselves.

They could have easily been looking back at me with my bike, helmet and gloves and thinking I looked like a stereotypical cyclist!

As I cycled I wondered how many of us emulate classical stereotypes: the Biker type, Racer type, Farmer type, Rich type, etc.

I wondered what was wrong with just being our authentic, natural selves. I remembered when I had emulated various stereotypes in my past and how much fun it was. I remember spending a huge amount of money attempting to play the astronomer type, with the photographer type coming in a close second.

It later occurred to me, watching our girl play FBI agent at home, that we learn and desire to emulate at an early age. Some of us want to be a fireman, others a ball player, or an astronaut or the other various stereotypes. We see these types and images and something about them calls to us and compels us to subscribe and attempt to act out and live through these models.

Is it merely human nature, programming, or something else that lures us down this path? To be honest, I really don't have an answer. Since it's a global phenomenon, however, I think its part of the learning cycle and human evolution. It's bound to play out for many people.

Let's say, for a moment, that through my words I paint a picture of a new type and it appeals to you. Won't you act upon it? I think it's natural to gravitate towards something that looks and seems like it will make you feel better.

Reading these words may begin to get confusing. Where are the lines, rules and boundaries on all this? Is it wrong to dream or want to emulate? I hate to disappoint you, but I don't have black and white answers to those questions. You are going to have to develop your own boundaries. You'll also need to remain flexible as your dreams will change as you grow older; trapping yourself in old dreams will surely lead to disappointment.

My intent is to get you to take some time to think about yourself and whether you're emulating a stereotype and if you care about your individuality and who you might be if you weren't acting like someone else.

Later in this book I will attempt to lure you into a mental exercise of inventorying the material and spiritual parts of your life. This exercise will help you to learn a great deal about yourself and how to use certain tools in order to secure a better, happier future. Remember, hindsight is 20/20!

Personally, I think that living a stable life while also pursuing fun activities is perfectly acceptable. If you feel that your life is lacking fun, picking something that appeals to you and escaping to it might bring some pep to your step. It's all about balance and not taking anything too far.

Our dreams and goals change as we develop and grow older. As older interests fade, new interests replace them. Interests can be cyclic; I am currently on my third cycle concerning photography.

Reconciling what you want and what is compatible with your life is perhaps one of the most difficult challenges we face. I love astronomy; however, I also seem to require more rest these days. I also have a family now, so that is where I devote most of my time. If I were to force myself to pursue this hobby despite the reality of my life, it would end up being a lose-lose situation for everyone involved. This is a difficult area in which to achieve awareness. Each of us has to assess the cost and impacts of our choices and actions. Many people wear themselves down trying to cram everything into their lives. In addition, many of us are tempted to think more of ourselves than the other people in our life. This failure to consider the feelings and needs of others will come back to haunt us, causing problems and disruptions. Balance within your entire circle is critical to your happiness.

If I have a main point I want to get across in this chapter, it is that it's okay to have dreams and that we should take time to balance our dreams against the reality of our lives. If we think it through, they can co-exist. I'd also encourage you to consider that getting everything we want is not always good for us. Sometimes what we want will negatively effect us, too much of a good thing can also become mundane.

Living Our Lies

Nope, it's not a typo. You might have thought the title was supposed to be living our lives instead of living our lies and, in a twisted way, it does refer to living a life of lies.

I guess it might make some of you uncomfortable to talk about living lies. It might feel like nails down a chalkboard or that queasy feeling you get when someone tells you what the hot dog you're eating is really made of.

Some people feel nothing in these type of conversations; they simply smile and take a bigger bite of the proverbial hot dog. While my initial intent was to make you feel a little queasy, at this point I'd like you to embrace the notion of living lies for a moment.

A Mind for Life

I'll confess that writing this book is really fun at times - expanding thoughts, dealing with contradictions - it can really be exciting. I have tried to throw away the rules and that may open me up to scrutiny. Please remember, however, that my real intent for this book is to help you see and embrace different ways of thinking. I am hoping to open your mind up, to allow you to view life and its events through new eyes, to bring you a greater awareness of programming and to enable you to customize that programming to be more individually efficient.

With that said, let's talk about the upshots of living the lie! Many of us find ourselves without direction in our lives. This may sound horrible; however, it is the reality for 90% of us at some point during our lives. Furthermore, often when we feel life is good and full of direction it's because we have subscribed to a particular thought or program, engaged in its execution and feel snug and comfy in the womb it creates.

All of this has an eerie similarity and parallel to the movie "The Matrix"; check it out sometime if you haven't already. In summary, the programming feels good when it's flowing through us and running well. Let's be honest, you could subscribe to a sequence of great programs and die a very happy person. There are good programs and bad programs out there but more often than not we are attracted to the programs that promise too much for too little.

What happens, however, if we don't subscribe to those programs? We could spend a lot of time thinking about this - there are millions of possibilities. It's easier, therefore, to generalize these possibilities into three major categories:

1.) Subscribe to the most common programs available and live them out.

2.) Create your own programs, which are either modified standard programs from above or totally customized ones, and live them out.

3.) Choose nothing and just live life as it comes.

While the third option may seem appalling to some people, I want to focus on it for a moment. I wish I could tell you the story behind how I got here; however, because it involves people close to me, I can't. I'll summarize by saying that someone I know was choosing a variant of this third option. They were choosing nothing and, in my opinion, going nowhere.

You might think that a person who chooses nothing is bound to go nowhere and that is a definite possibility. When you choose nothing other people will choose for you. You might think that choosing this option is illogical, or the view of lazy or dumb people and, ultimately, the choice made by the people society has labeled failures. There is a lot of negative thought surrounding this choice.

Consider, however, a perfectly smart person who lives day to day, chooses quickly and smartly among the opportunities that present themselves and follows life where it leads with a keen common sense and, ultimately, with success? How do we rationalize that possibility?

I think one could argue that the person in the latter example has really employed option two and created their own program of not subscribing to programs and living between the lines (of code).

If you wonder where I'm headed with this, ask no more! It may be helpful to reverse the order of the above options and view them as a process and/or framework. If we find that we have chosen option three and are going nowhere and doing nothing, we may want to switch gears and employ option one. The important thing is to find a program or group of programs that appeal to us and then run with them.

Earlier in the book, we discussed change and the act of taking baby steps towards what will later become a major change. Moving from option three (the negative version, where you're getting nowhere fast and feel lost) to option one will get you on a better path. I remember a day during my first week of electronics school where my teacher said that everything he would say to us for awhile would be a lie because that was essential to us ultimately understanding the truth. To that end, perhaps living a lie until we can find the truth makes sense. In the absence of truth and real direction, the lies can successfully fill the space if we choose them using our common sense. One downside of this is you may tend to have moments where you feel like something is missing! That faint hollow feeling will always be there until we feel that we are living a life of purpose.

You can start by finding one or more models and beginning to emulate them. If you aren't satisfied with the models then move to option two and start modifying them to suit your own needs. I'll caution you to exercise good sense when doing this. For instance, you can't attempt to emulate the model of an athlete and then do nothing athletic or endeavor to imitate a millionaire if you have no money or capital. It simply won't work and you will most likely fail. Therefore, when choosing a model, you must first look at what you need to make the model work and see if you have what it takes!

Most well-known models work for the people that successfully adopt and then adapt to them. Most people sail through the adoption but never successfully adapt. It's like getting a heart transplant only to have your body reject the organ. The rosier side of emulation is that it will help you to feel busy and engaged. You will, however, still have to deal with that faint emptiness I referenced before. Emulation will always be just that - an emulation - real fulfillment only comes as you introduce a factor of reality that helps make all of the strings and seams disappear.

You have to choose the model or program that is right for you. Most times entry-level programs are the best choice as they allow you to begin without building a foundation. If you successfully execute these and wish to move on, you can always move to the intermediate level of programs within that same model.

Assume that all models are made up of programs. The biker type, for example, contains programs on how to dress, how to act, what bike to ride, what friends to have, what things to do, etc.

People sometimes create their own stereotypes using a batch of different programs. The yuppie type, for example, is a newer stereotype that gained notability in the late 80's and 90's. You can think of models as stereotypes and references that you access using your life experiences and surroundings. While these ideas may be obvious to some of you, let's discuss them a little further in order to ensure that we are all on the same page.

I am going to dive fairly deep into this idea in order to more clearly illustrate some essential points. Consider a situation where an average person is feeling lost, directionless and as if they aren't heading to a better place any time soon. They are sporting quite a few extra pounds, have grown tired and stagnant in their career and feel like their current relationship isn't working. Sounds like a dreary place to be in life, doesn't it?

This person could choose to adopt the following models/programs!

They could emulate the gym-person model. If you join a gym and conduct a little people watching, sooner or later you'll find a person who comes in, does a committed and fairly intense workout 3 - 4 times a week and looks moderately fit. If you see someone start and follow through, you can literally watch his or her transformation.

They don't look like the other people you see at the gym - the supermodel athletic types – that model isn't very realistic for beginners. Instead, the person is on their way to being in shape. Someone who completes a daily exercise routine is an example of a good entry-level model.

Other people at the gym, sometimes comically called "wannabe's", are only there because they have nothing else to do. They are the ones who are only working out with 5 lbs. of weight, never sweat, never stay long and only walk slowly and briefly on the treadmill. They really don't look all that fit, unless they are genetically blessed with a thinner athletic frame. That model isn't going to work for the person in our example either.

Yep, unfortunately, the program they need is the one that actually requires them to do real and increasingly challenging exercises until they find a point that allows for maintenance. This model will allow our person to eat, in moderation, many of the things they like and be able to work those calories off through exercise. They will attain a level of fitness that allows them to walk up five flights of stairs without experiencing a heart attack or shortness of breath.

By following this model, working with a personal trainer every few months to adjust their routine and sticking to the workouts just like the gym person they're trying to emulate, they will eventually end up looking and feeling a whole lot better, despite their initial struggles.

Let's stick with the programming model and say that an entry level set of programs has built you up to a certain point. Perhaps you started by walking on a treadmill and lifting small weights. As you progress, you started to intermittently jog while you're on the treadmill and increased the size of the weights you were lifting. After two months you are actually emulating the model you chose. Don't immediately try to emulate the person we described earlier - you'll probably seriously hurt yourself.

Okay, so we've now chosen one model/program that targets a third of the issues that our previously hopeless person needed to address.

Let's tackle their job situation next!

I find it really helps to sit down and write notes on what's bugging you and what you want out of life. See the chapter entitled Needs for more information.

In this scenario I might start by making a list of what you do and do not like about your current job. Follow that up with a list addressing what would need to change about your job and/or yourself in order to feel good about continuing to work there. After you've made these lists, set them aside!

Next, make a list of new jobs that match your skill set and you feel would reenergize and excite you. Think of people you know and admire and see if their job model appeals to you. Maybe it's your office manager friend with the cool jazzy tie who is always sporting a smile and frequently says, "I love my job!" Using these things as starting points, make a list and choose the three job options that appeal to you the most.

As you look at your lists, explore the pros and cons of each option and then choose the one that you like the best and consider what it might take to pursue that option successfully. Ask yourself if you need training, if you have or are able to obtain the necessary tools, if there are openings in the field and if your expectations are realistic. Then look at whether there are sub-goals that can steer you towards your ultimate goal. A helpful thought process to use in this situation is called the elegant solution. If you employ it correctly you will be in a win-win situation. All you have to do is follow a set of actions that allow you to both make your current job work and be ready for a new job if you so choose.

You might be thinking that this sounds like a lot of work. Yes, it is. But remember, it usually takes hard work to get the most out of the things we want in life! Luck is luck - not a guarantee.

Yes, finding a solution to your job situation can be a job unto its own! Either buck up, deal with it, quit wasting time complaining and get moving or just give in, suck it up and stop whining about your current job. A person unwilling to seek and work for change doesn't deserve change! Feeling the tough love, aren't you? Smile!

Seriously though, explore your lists and develop a plan to improve your current job, find a new job or employ the elegant solution that allows you to do both and more. You need to aggressively attack this process, but don't to be afraid to fail and end up back at the drawing board. You may very well have to fail quite a few times before you achieve success.

Success is often a process of trial and error; if you initially fail, simply do some fine-tuning before you try again. Finding known, successful, proven programs will also help to keep you from having to reinvent the wheel. If you objectively evaluate your failures and make sensible adjustments you'll usually find success. One more word of caution: remember to set realistic goals - the most common reason for failure is unrealistic expectations and objectives.

The bottom line is that you'll either discover a way to revitalize your existing job by re-engaging, taking a leadership role in something you're passionate about, preparing for new opportunities, or you may also find a new job that changes things up. If all else fails, pick the model of someone who inspires you and work to emulate and make it successful for yourself.

The sum of your situation will manifest itself in all aspects of your life: your health, your wealth and your relationships!

Sometimes problems are really the result of other problems. For example, if you are down about the way you look and about your job, these feelings might project into your relationships. You may find that by simply looking better and spending more of your day feeling positive because you have a new handle on your job that you will also feel better in your free time.

The more pieces of your life you put together the more other problems will simply vaporize. It's true! A more positive outlook results in a more optimistic view about just about everything. When the chips are down, small things seem worse and are more aggravating. Even the smallest, stupidest things seem like huge mountains of aggravation!

Your relationship is also influenced by how your partner feels about you. This could be directly tied to your health, your job situation, the way those situations cause you to act and moods they produce. As you change, their view of you may change and, as a result, your feelings may change as well.

What about that relationship problem?

Well, I decided to address this issue last because many relationship problems are aggravated and worsened by other problems in your life. Furthermore, straightening out your own life can cause tension between you and the significant people in your life! You'll appear different and while this more positive you is a wonderful thing, others may not see it that way. They might resent these changes and wish you'd never gotten your act together.

I've seen men divorce women because they became more successful, aggressive and less afraid to work for what they wanted in life. I've seen women divorce men because they changed, became too energetic and wanted more from life. This might make you wonder why you should even try to change? You'll have to think about it and, above all, be sensitive to the ripple affect it may have. You can change your outlook on life and also not expect all of your friends and family to have a parade in your honor celebrating your accomplishments. Real, solid, good change sits quietly and comfortably inside yourself.

You might consider bringing your loved ones along for the ride and recommend that they read this book and employ some of the concepts discussed in it. You may want them to feel better as well, be happier, freer, etc. This is a perfectly natural response to the people you love and care about.

One of the hardest things you may find on your journey is that the people around you, many of whom you care about, can end up being a large part of what brings you down. I encourage you to try and help them; however, I also caution you to be extremely careful in your efforts. The act of bringing someone along with you will often be met with extreme resistance.

Some people hate optimists; they loathe and despise their existence. Often this is motivated by their belief that life is nothing more than a horrific journey they are forced to endure. It is for this reason that, elsewhere in this book, I have addressed methods of effective communication, influence and ways of bringing about change.

If you can convince those you love to join you on your journey - step by step, concept by concept, together - it may work. It will, however, make the journey more difficult and more likely to result in failure. If this happens, I encourage you digest the book yourself and try to re-approach if necessary.

Remember, while you may wish that other people would change their outlooks on life, it's not realistic for you to expect that they will! I'll repeat myself: good change will sit quietly and comfortably within yourself. If you are able to refrain from projecting your new outlook onto others you have become an extra special person.

Others may consider you to be pessimistic when you are suggesting change. Change is considered bad to many people and by asking them to change they feel you are implying that there is something wrong with them. Therefore, they view your request as negative, pessimistic and even insulting.

Okay, enough sidetracks, what about relationships already?

You'll find a common theme in the way I approach problems. If you hate the idea of sitting and writing things down, you may find this approach annoying. I know that all too well. I used to feel the same way; I did everything in my head. All I can tell you is that organized thought is far more powerful and effective than disorganized thought and writing things down has been a powerful aid in organizing, visualizing and addressing my own problems.

Therefore, I encourage you to write down the things in your life that bother you. Re-read the chapter on expectations and then examine your list for reasonable expectations and unreasonable expectations.

You might believe, at first, that the problems in your relationship are all the fault of your partner and that you are behaving perfectly. I guarantee, however, that is most likely not the case. The problems are almost always related to our unreasonable expectations for the people we are with. That, unto itself, is a powerful thought! We too often expect things of people that they simply aren't capable of and didn't promise to deliver and then hold them fully accountable for failing to meet our expectations.

Let's say you meet a troubled person, fall in love and feel certain that you can make them happy, wash all their problems away and lead them towards a better life. You may be a wonderful, loving, caring person who bends over backwards to give them the world only to find that they remain troubled and, ultimately, undesirable. The truth of a scenario like this is that the troubled person probably hasn't changed at all and is simply being the same person they were when you first met them. They may have done nothing wrong; they have simply been themselves. Your poor judgment, however, is likely to cause them to be more miserable when you turn around and abandon them.

The difference, in this scenario, is you! You changed throughout the entire process. You probably saw them for who they were and decided you could make their life better. You accepted them under the premise that you could change them. You tried and you failed. You got frustrated. You got down on them. You gave up on them. And then you decided you didn't want them anymore.

That's a tough cycle to endure and a bitter pill to swallow isn't it? This is why it's critical to start with your expectations of a relationship before even beginning to worry about your partner. You may have heard the expression that states you can't be happy in a relationship until you yourself are able to make and keep your own self happy.

A Mind for Life

I am reminded of a young lady I know who was chasing a boy who already had a girlfriend. I tried to tell her that if she were that guy's girlfriend she would hate any girl that was flirting with or trying to take her boyfriend away. Even if she put that aside and lured the boy away from his girlfriend, I told her, what would that say about the kind of guy he was? This young lady, however, was certain they were meant to be together and that all she needed to do was make him hers and everything would work out. They started hanging out, the boy kept his girlfriend and she still chases after him. The boy is probably wrong for hanging out with another girl, but he also hasn't exactly hidden it from her. It's right out there for this young lady to see and decide whether she still wants to pursue the relationship. In her mind, however, she sees the situation differently. Eventually she will probably see the situation for what it really is - an illusion she alone created and pursued. Who will take the blame when the reality of the situation is ultimately revealed?

We all too often have the expectation that it takes some other person or thing to make us happy. It's my belief that the capacity to be happy comes from within ourselves, but we are seldom programmed or educated on how to create and manage our own self-sustaining happiness.

So, as usual, I've been jumping around on you. Let's refocus on our main objective.

Assume you've read the whole book and spent a few years reprogramming and you now make that list again and it contains very few things about your relationship for which you're accountable. Let's, for the sake of argument, say that the person you thought you knew has really changed. Perhaps when you met them they were self-sufficient, slim, neat, well dressed and interesting and they have now turned into a smelly, mean, lazy slob.

At this point you must determine whether you believe that these issues are circumstantial, will change of their own course, can be changed with help or are likely to never change. Your next questions should revolve around your ability to accept who they are now and whether doing so would be the right thing for you.

You also have to take a long, hard, honest look at yourself. If your heart is no longer with this person, the sad truth may be that you need to let them go rather than continue living a lie.

It's important to understand that two people may be very good people and simply grow apart and take different paths. This happens a lot and many people in this situation simply don't make a change. There is not necessarily a right or wrong way to deal with this; many times spiritual beliefs and the consideration for your children come into play. I think if two people can rekindle what attracted them to each other in the beginning and are both willing to make some changes they may be able to meet in the middle and love again. One great way to begin rekindling the fire is to sit down and flip through your wedding album.

I personally went through a situation where I ignored my own true wants for many years only to finally realize that I needed to make a real change. That experience gave me a lot of insight. It's really tough sometimes and the heart cannot always be ruled by pure logic. For example, logically speaking you could determine that the relationship you are in will destroy you and still find that in your core heart it's impossible for you to terminate it.

Giving up on a relationship can generate tremendous feelings of guilt and personal failure. Pressure from your family may play a role in your decision making and feelings. The struggles with changing a relationship can be intense, extremely emotional and, ultimately, profoundly life-changing. It's insane that we, as people, make decisions like these all the time!

I would love to give you some magic pearl of wisdom but all I can tell you is that if you can't make alterations and you know in your heart that nothing will change, then the next best thing to do is to sit down and talk to your partner and tell them how you feel. I am guessing, however, that they probably already know at this point or you would have done that already.

Communication is extremely important in a relationship. Bottling things up and hiding your true feelings are detrimental to a relationship. It's a double edge sword, however, because if we aren't careful about how we express ourselves our words can cause irreversible damage. Your loved one will never forget you telling them things like "you're just ugly," or "you're a horrible, mean person." Words like those, while seemingly mild for some, are inspired by pure anger for others. Their effects can last decades and are often never truly forgiven. I find it helpful to write my thoughts down and sit with them for a bit before sharing them. Many times I even throw them away because the act of writing them down and reviewing them brings me clarity and allows me to find a better way of dealing with my emotions.

The truth is that our words hurt and so we should try our very best to choose them carefully. This unto itself is a very important self-awareness to gain - what you say matters and it is rare to get a chance to take it back and do it over! When we seriously hurt another person, "sorry" doesn't really work. That hurt will rattle around inside them for an eternity. Elsewhere in this book I'll talk about betrayal and forgiveness; they are also important subjects to consider when it comes to relationships.

If, after talking through things with your partner, you have found that your differences are irreconcilable or, despite repeated attempts to reconcile, that nothing has changed then you might decide it's time to move on.

One thing I think is important to consider and really helps you know if you are making the right decision when it comes to ending a relationship is to imagine and visualize your life without your partner. Try it on for size in your mind. If you try it on and it looks and feels great then you probably will feel more assured with your decision. If, however, it feels wrong then perhaps you need to go back through the cycle again and determine if you are the one that is off track.

Only you can make the ultimate decision. If I could say one thing about relationships, it's that perpetual delays can result in lost happiness for both people. If you are not right for each other and you stay together than you are both going to be very unhappy. It also can impact all the people around you, including your friends, family and children.

In an ideal world we would be able to be more deliberate about choosing the people to whom we want to be close. In the real world, however, hormones and many other factors that we can't control draw us to people that are not always right for us.

A Mind for Life

This brings me back to the concept of emulations and lies. Frequently, the programs we choose to follow in our relationships fail. This failure is probably due to the complex and dynamic nature of human beings. The person you fall in love with today may become a very different person seven years from now. Often people resent others when they change in ways they don't appreciate. Instead, I encourage you to consider whose problem it really is, yours or theirs and then find a reasonably intelligent way to deal with it. If you go back to the chapter concerning life-cycles, you will see that we all transform several times throughout our lifetime.

A difficult question to answer for many is if your heart is not in a relationship, who really benefits? I suggest you start by working to see if your love can be restored or revitalized. Telling someone you love them when you really don't can be very damaging to both them and you.

The ramifications of emulations in relationships are huge. We can also have selective sight in emulations. We see, for instance, our grandparents who were married for an eternity and always seemed happy, full of cheer and love when we visited and subscribe to that program. What we don't realize, however, is that we were seeing the best version of their relationship. In reality, they faced and overcame many struggles and often put their own needs and happiness on the back burner out of their love for each other.

Either through work or luck they were able to adapt to each other's changes. Perhaps they grew together, instead of apart, as many married couples seem to do these days. Perhaps their beliefs and faiths are what eternally bound them together. The challenge with adopting programming is that we need to remain aware of all the dynamics of the models and programs we choose to ensure that they are truly well suited for us. We must also learn to modify and adapt these programs on the fly. These are some of the reasons that it is so important that we understand who our partners really are, and vice versa.

While I'd love to talk more about this, we do need to return to where we started and bring closure to the concept of a life of lies! Before we do, I'll share one more thought with you. Be very careful when you try to incorporate emulations into your relationships. Relationships are a part of life where the hollow feeling emulations often can become very destructive. Who, after all, wants to fake love?

Earlier, I walked you through some actions that had our hypothetical person significantly changing their appearance, their health, their job and even their relationships. That's a lot of changes and, in most cases; they would take months and years to cover. Reprogramming never stops; it requires a lifetime of work.

Hopefully we've now seen instances where living lies can be very useful or very harmful. We've explored some of the mischief that may occur when we are living lies and emulating others. We've also seen how prolific life changes can come about as a result of being more aware of our programming and selectively choosing which programs to adopt and modify.

If you really stopped and considered all that we have covered in these pages, you may begin to get a strong appetite for what A Mind For Life philosophy can do for you. It's not magic; it's work, but the rewards for your efforts are like no other rewards you can experience in life. That's because achieving and learning to sustain real happiness is absolutely priceless! I'd rather live twenty years happily than one hundred years like most people do. Something to consider, isn't it?

Oh, and about that haunting hollow feeling I referenced? I have some thoughts about how to transcend it in the chapters that follow. Remember Option 2? Learning to alter the programs for more compatible and successful existence brings our game to a new level!

It's never too late to make changes!

Wow - looking ahead and looking back - the distances appear to be about equal! You have already journeyed far!

The Road In
Mark Abraham
Texas 2006

In the distance we see a destination and the lines lead us there with certainty. Often when we arrive we see another horizon and another destination. Our mood is all about how we see the next horizon and whether it's an adventure or just another long haul!

Decisions

By the time you finish reading A Mind for Life, even without this chapter, you will be equipped with new ideas, thought patterns and techniques which will help you make better decisions.

I do, however, want to take it a step further and talk about some additional techniques which may also help you make decisions throughout your life.

Some decision-making is simply based on intuition; it's a non-event. If a decision needs to be made quickly usually you will experience some unconscious thoughts and perhaps access some memories and then a decision will spew forth. Other times decision making is very laborious, painful, long and scary. Often the decision will be made with great hesitation and without any confidence.

You don't have to make all of your decisions on your own. With the advent of the internet and social networking there are tons of people who have probably asked and responded to the question or decision you're contemplating. I love to use Google and the internet as research tools whenever I have a problem. I'd say nine out of ten times I weigh the opinions and past experiences of others before I make my own decision.

Furthermore, you should decide which solution makes you the most comfortable. It's important to realize, when we are making decisions, that there are often many options available to us. Finding the path that feels good to you is important. As you are considering your options, you should look down each path and decide whether you are able to live with your choice regardless of the outcome.

And I had you thinking that making decisions was all about choosing the right path! Smile! Hard as it is to deal with, we make wrong decisions all the time. The thought of making a bad decision for the right reasons may seem like we are unnecessarily complicating things. However, regret is one of those horrible emotions we experience in life and we can limit it if we think a little more before we take action.

Don't underestimate the value of a parent or friend in helping you make decisions - especially if they have been through the situation themselves. Even if their decision looks like it was a bad one, you can learn something by talking with them if they are willing. It's funny how afraid we get when it comes to asking for help. Our ego somehow twists us into thinking that we are too smart to seek help. It's amazing how we forget to consider our pride with regard to failure. I am always astounded that people are willing to ignore help and resources that are available to them when they make decisions. I think it's because, inside, we just want to decide the way we want to without any regard for the consequences.

Imagine if you had leveraged the wisdom of others to help you make decisions throughout your life. How much better off would you be? Unfortunately, we are often too proud to think this way. There is something divisive about the amount of arrogance we portray in our youth. The beatings we take from our inevitable failures, however, usually cause us to gain humility and wisdom. It's how we evolve!

Its mind-blowing to think how much of our lives we spend relearning the lessons others have already learned for us. Our arrogance is simply incomprehensible! Are we forever doomed to this snail like evolution, or can we gain the awareness and accelerate to new levels of existence?

Another useful tool in decision-making is to virtually try on the decision in your mind. Imagine you've made the decision and consider all of the good and bad that will result from it. Google "I bought a condo in Florida" for example and notice the wide array of results the search yields. You'll find everything from someone's horror story to another's experience living a wonderful life in a condo in the Sunshine State.

As a part of this virtual trial method I also suggest that you ask lots of questions. What am I likely to feel one year after buying this condo? Will it still seem special or will it just be the place I live and pay the bill for? What will it really cost? The idea is to imagine what it's really like - as if you had already made the decision and are now living with the results. This technique also works well if you're questioning a relationship. Think about what your life would be like if you were moving forward on your own. You'll be amazed at the thoughts you'll have and the new problems you may uncover.

Map out your decision and its consequences on paper or in your head. When there are lots of variables I use paper or a computer with a word processor. It just helps to organize and see the problem and its results more clearly.

What if questions also work well! Ask yourself how a small change here or there would affect the result of your decision. This will help you tailor your decision and plans around that decision in order to optimize the result and achieve success beyond what others have experienced.

Don't be afraid to model negative scenarios as well. In our condo example, consider what would happen if the area you were targeting was re-zoned or hit by a hurricane. These questions might lead you to choose a different place or urge you to obtain the right insurance coverage. They might even cause you to back out of the whole deal if you realize that the cost of insurance doesn't fit in your budget.

Modeling extreme scenarios can also be helpful. Consider extreme options as you make your decision. What would happen if you threw a large sum of money at it or changed the whole way you do business? Would those extreme options solve the problem or simply create new ones? Perhaps, for example, a leader of a country declares martial law because he believes that keeping everyone locked in their homes will end the civil distress the country has been experiencing. That's an extreme decision and it will have extreme consequences. The fear such a decision might create amongst its citizens could, for instance, impact that countries' economy and have other long-term consequences.

Another technique I like to use is the problem slicing method. The idea is to keep slicing your problem in half until the windows of possibilities are small enough that the answer to the problem jumps out at you. This is a troubleshooting technique I learned in the Army and it has helped me solve problems more quickly.

For example, let's say your house is a mess and you just discovered company is coming over in ten minutes. Deciding to focus on the lower half of the house because that's where your guests will first arrive slices the mess in half. By looking at it again you decide that on the lower floor they will pass through a hallway and then go to your sitting room, this reduces your focus in half again. Now the problem is small enough that you are able to take action and save yourself from embarrassment. It's a silly example, but it's very illustrative of what slicing your problems in half can accomplish.

Another quick example is a scenario in which you have laid one thousand yards of extension cords only to get to the end and find no power. After you have ensured the cords are plugged in, go to the middle and see if you have power. If you find power there, then go to the ¾ mark and try again, progressing until you find the faulty connection.

As you can see there are many ways to approach decision-making. When decisions get difficult I consider them to be problems and apply problem-solving logic to them.

A Mind for Life

To have confidence in decisions that you deem tough, you'll need to spend some time and effort considering them. Seek the opinion of others, place yourself in other people's shoes and consider the impact your decision will have on others. Try virtually wearing the decision in your mind as if you've already made it and are now moving forward. Seek to slice your problems in half and reduce their scope.

Last but not least, you must to decide if these words are of value and use to you! Smile! If they are you'll have to make an effort in order to gain the awareness to recognize their utility and to inject these concepts into your daily thought processes.

Fitness

As with most of the chapters in this book, you'll find this chapter to be short and geared more towards commentary rather than an in-depth discussion.

I believe our bodies are a part of our minds. There are so many ways to illustrate this concept, but let's focus on just a few.

How you feel often correlates to your level of fitness. If you are heavy then it becomes tiring to drag yourself around each day. If you get really heavy then it can begin to get difficult to do even simple things like get out of bed, climb a flight of stairs or even to tie your shoes.

While many people consider working out or strenuous activity to be stressful, many others find that exercise is extremely helpful in releasing their stress. If you've ever had the wonderment of experiencing a workout high while exercising, you know it can become addictive; you try to repeat that high every time you workout.

Workout regimens produce many benefits – benefits that many people fail to consider. Not only do we get to look better, we also get to feel better. I feel more relaxed after a workout. I also feel good about having taken time to take care of myself. Fitness is an investment in you.

Maintaining a level of fitness promotes confidence and improves our mental health. I often find it easier to work through my problems while I'm working out.

I'd like to tell you that I'm the spitting image of health and fitness, but I'm not. I have, however, focused on my fitness a lot more over the past few years. I invest significantly more time and energy into it now than I did in the past.

In the world we live in, it becomes all too easy to set our health aside in favor of the many other attractions competing for our attention.

So here is my food for thought for you in this chapter. Take some time to consider your health. Take a walk, not only will you get some exercise, you'll also get some fresh air and time to reflect, clean out your mind and enjoy some pretty scenery. Simply walking for thirty minutes 3-4 times a week would be a significant step in the right direction.

If you get the walking down, attempt something a little more physical, provided your doctor supports the activity. Perhaps going to the gym, riding a bike or engaging in a team sport is the right activity for you.

Watch what you eat, there are a lot of bad foods out there that are approved for consumption. Many of the FDA approvals assume that people are consuming certain foods in moderation, but the reality is that many of us consume way more of these things than the test cases allow for.

Being conscious of the way foods and drinks impact us is an important part of becoming self-aware.

A simple health log is very useful in correlating the things we consume with changes in our health. I've learned some very interesting things this way. For instance, I discovered that the artificial mint flavoring found in chewing gum and breath mints gives me migraine headaches. I also learned that heavily synthetic perfumes and colognes cause me to experience major headaches and nausea.

I learned that one company's cola product gives me a runny nose, while another's does not. Unfortunately, the latter company's cola sometimes causes me to experience headaches. If I drink coffee in the mid-afternoon I get a headache, but if I consume it before noon or after 5 pm I have no problems. I also determined that eating red meat hurts my teeth. Logging what you have eaten when you feel bad will help you build awareness about what's causing your symptoms - you will begin to notice the patterns. Currently, I keep notes in my phone since I always have it with me. You'll be amazed at how many of the foods you love are causing you to feel badly. Things like wine and beer, for instance, can cause your nose to run or cause you to feel stuffy. I have to laugh because they obviously have other side effects as well!

The Internet contains a lot of great information about healthier living; subscribe to a newsletter or two. You'll be surprised at what you may learn.

I once learned about some herbal remedies that can be used to reverse gum disease. I took them and not only did I get rid of and reverse the gum problems I had, but a large scar on my leg from when I was only 14 opened up again, healed and became almost invisible. This was over twenty years after the original incident. My doctor couldn't believe it. There are lots of helpful natural remedies out there. Be careful, however, many of these remedies don't live up to their hype and some can even hurt you. Also, some remedies may help one person and harm another; we're all different. Your body is a temple so carefully read up before you take anything; consulting your physician first is also highly advisable.

Just as you log what makes you feel bad, you can also log what herbs and dietary changes make you feel better. Every person's physiology is different; therefore, it takes time to find what works best for YOU. By recording your observations you'll find patterns that can help you identify the long-term changes you need to make in order to feel and look healthier.

If you're having a hard time beginning an exercise program or diet, keeping a log and set of slow steps and goals can be extremely helpful. If you are having a hard time on your own, work with your doctor to formulate a plan that helps you to slowly step into a healthier life. I will say this; nobody can do the work for you.

Fitness

Cutting down on bad food and regular exercise are the two primary ways you can improve your health and level of fitness.

Personally, I started by walking. Once I was walking for one hour five days a week, I joined a gym. At the gym, I began by burning 200 calories a visit and worked my way to 800 calories a visit over the course of one year. Steps - small steps - are the secret. With each step you will slowly work your way towards the goals you really want to achieve.

I fell in love with the stair-mill of all things! This machine tells you how many flights of stairs you've climbed. I started off with 10 floors, then 20, 40, 60, 80 and so forth. I started thinking about how tall famous buildings were so I could climb the equivalent of the Empire State Building (about 103 Floors), The World Trade Center (about 108) and, finally, the Sears Tower (about 114). Then I went a little crazy and climbed the equivalent of both towers of the World Trade Center back to back (220 floors). Next, I climbed 240 floors. Then I decided I wanted to climb six miles of stairs and so one day I set out to do it. Ninety minutes later I had climbed 300 stories and about 6.3 miles of stairs.

The second secret to achieving your goals is to make sure the changes you've made stick with you for a lifetime. Find a balance in your lifestyle that is healthy and reasonably maintainable. If you're completely dependent on a gym and daily workout routine to maintain your weight, sooner or later you're likely to fail. Working out so that you can eat what you want works for a while, but it is likely to fail in the long run. These days I'm striving to maintain a balance of regular exercise and a balanced diet.

A Mind for Life

A few years ago, after I got so fit from climbing all of those stairs, I took a hike up a mountain and was literally able to run up the mountain trail with my camera gear. I was amazed at how easy it seemed. It felt great!

In conclusion, your body is part of your mental being. Whether it's physiologically linked to the levels of chemicals in your blood, the ease or difficulty with which you breathe and how well you digest foods, or psychologically linked to the way you feel about yourself and your appearance, you'll notice a vast difference if you seek and are successful in improving your health.

Part of developing A Mind For Life is developing a level of fitness that allows you to keep your mind off of your body and appearance.

Owning Our Mistakes

What does it really mean to own your mistakes? I bet most of you would answer this question differently. Here's my take.

The first step in truly owning your mistakes is to acknowledge that you messed up. As I've previously stated, we often don't even take this first step as we choose to blame others, instead of ourselves, for the bad things that occur in our lives. I contend that there is very little good luck and bad luck in life. Instead, there is planning for success and failing to plan for success, the latter of which usually results in failure.

Once we acknowledge that we've made a mistake, we must accept and deal with the consequences. This step can be hard – it forces us to acknowledge our mistake over and over again. The more difficult and impacting the consequences are, the more we're tempted to blame others. The proverbial cry of "Why Me?" and self-pity parties frequently occur during these times.

Many people may believe that this is the final step of the cycle. Once we've accepted the consequences of our actions and repaired the damage caused by the mistake, we feel the cycle is complete. I disagree. Mistakes often result in us feeling a lasting bitterness. Therefore, scrubbing the negative emotional residue from our mind is a key part of gaining total ownership over our mistakes.

There are different ways a person can go about this. One of my favorite methods is to attempt to find the good in the bad. I often do this by feeling grateful that I survived the mistake and appreciative that I learned a valuable lesson. If you feel you truly learned a lesson and are better equipped to prevent yourself from falling into the same hole again, you can start to change your negative emotions into positive ones.

Honestly, I've turned many bad things into positive references throughout the course of my life. Think of it like a pendulum. You can use the momentum you gain from swinging low to propel you back to the top. The secret is to jump off the swing when it's reached its highest point.

This may sound strange and crazy; so let me provide you with a more realistic example. It's not my favorite illustration, but it's the one that comes to mind right now. Consider what happens when someone pushes you down really hard. Have you ever seen someone take a devastating blow and been sure that they will be down for the count? The last thing anyone expects is for the person who looks down and out to pop right back up and deliver an even more devastating blow to his opponent. Part of what makes that second blow even more devastating is the fact that it is a complete surprise to their opponent, whose guard is usually down.

Often winning comes down to one, small, unexpected burst of energy focused for maximum delivery and perfect timing when people are least expecting it. Think about how many great things happen in just that way! For this person, getting knocked down was an opportunity; it opened up a window for surprise that led to them winning the bout.

Opportunities often arise when we least expect it. While the analogy I provided is a bit extreme, it does illustrate how we often walk with our eyes and mind so focused on a limited slice of the field of view ahead, we miss everything that is to the side, above and below our line of sight.

How many people have laid the foundation of their fortunes during bad economic downturns? Some people just see these downturns as investment opportunities.

In order to truly own our mistakes we must complete the whole cycle. This doesn't mean, however, that we'll never think about our mistakes again. The goal is to be at a point where you no longer feel bitterness. Instead, you feel knowing, enlightened and armed with the awareness to not let your mistakes set you back and take your attention away from the better part of the big game called life! It's hard to hit a home run when we're preoccupied at the plate thinking about our last strikeout!

In summary, by acknowledging that we have failed, making good on these failures and cleansing our minds of the residue of bitterness we are able to move forward. When we do this, looking back at our mistakes is a positive exercise! We can more successfully navigate the future. We then complete the cycle and what was once bad becomes wisdom!

Pole Coon
Mark Abraham
Paola, Kansas 2004

It's okay to clown around and have some fun in life. If we don't have fun and laughter in our lives then we cry a river of tears while our spirit dwindles. Are we just hanging on?

Expectations

In some ways, this is the granddaddy of all the chapters I've written. So give it your full attention!

Sometimes people never have the conversations they could or should have with each other. Sometimes it's difficult to know whether we should reach out when we see someone we love feeling troubled or down. We fear they may desire to be left alone to ponder what's bothering them. Ironically, the people who love and care for them the most often feel that they are the least capable of helping. Furthermore, even if we do attempt to help, our offers are often rejected.

I've spent a lot of time thinking about the best ways to help someone. Everyone has their own free will and opinions – I've tried far too many times to force someone to see things differently. Now I prefer the safer and more effective route of simply offering my assistance, without expecting my offer to be accepted. I try to introduce them to the alternative ways of thinking that I've been exploring over the past several years.

When we pass by someone and sense his or her unhappiness we are faced with a difficult decision. Should we reach out or not? Thinking that it's unnatural for someone to be unhappy is a bit self-centered of us. Optimists often dislike people who feel down; they think they are contaminating their own happiness. Some people are so self-centered that they run from sad people as if they are diseased. They tend to forget their own experiences with sadness.

On the other hand, people who are feeling sad often reject offers of help because they can't see past their misery and suffering. They often believe their unhappiness is justified! So they too selfishly hold on to their emotions.

It's obvious that life is full of highs and lows and I think that's perfectly natural. I believe everyone is accountable for his or her own happiness and it is up to them to choose how he or she wish to deal with the challenges they face in life. I do believe, however, that we can help each other. In fact, it's mostly through interaction with others and life events that we form our own perspectives. A realist will look at each event and find both the good and the bad.

I frequently hear people ask: "How could God do this?" This is one of the most frequently misplaced questions since so much of what happens to us is the result of our own choices. We fail to realize that God gives us the gift of thought and through this tool we make both poor and wise decisions in how we live our life. I believe the greatest gift God gives us is free will.

Expectations

If you know, for example, that a volcano resides where you want to live and you willingly move there anyway only to have it erupt and wipe you out, do you blame God or own up to poor decision-making? God gave you the wisdom to know that he placed a volcano there and he gave you the gift of choice. It's true that hindsight can be 20/20; however, many times it's our own impatience and overly optimistic natures that lead to the bad things we experience.

We often expect God and others to do everything perfectly. These expectations create a lot of unhappiness. Not only do expectations impact the materialistic side of life, they actually profoundly impact our spirituality. I believe this is the most important part of our life.

I believe expectations are the pivot point in determining our spirituality. Reconciling our expectations with reality can often be an intense battle.

Expectations are one of the key ingredients of our morality. We expect everyone to abide by all commonly accepted laws. We expect everyone to not hurt, kill, steal or betray each other, along with a myriad of other laws.

The problem is that people disappoint us and break these laws every day. We then spend lots of time and effort dealing with these people. This often causes us to begin to doubt people in general.

The issue is whether we expect too much and, in my opinion, that question is not easy to answer. If you lower your expectations many people will take that as an invitation to loosen up their behavior and break the rules more often. On the other hand, if you expect everyone to follow every law, every day, you are setting yourself up for sure disappointment. It simply won't happen that way in the real world. In addition to being a tremendous source of disappointment, these high expectations cause us to feel victimized by the people we assumed wouldn't break the law when they do.

All of this is an invitation for us to employ our common sense. I, for instance, expect people to abide by the law. I know, however, that many will not and therefore don't get overly disappointed or hurt when people fail to comply with the law.

I hope and pray that everyone will find a path that allows them to live, happily and peacefully, within the laws of society. I know and expect, however, that many will fail, and I pray that they find the hope, wisdom and the strength to do better next time. We all have failings in life, and even though some of us believe we are perfect and never fail, everyone does. To even think you are faultless in this world is a failure unto itself, and it surely means you have wronged others with your self-elevation and notions of perfection. People who think this way have little compassion and are often very bitter and unhappy.

Then what should we expect from life, its purpose and meaning, and God's role in our fate? These are great questions! I believe God grants us life and the ability to choose our beliefs.

Sometimes we waste these gifts with our poor choices. Sometimes other's lives abruptly end and cause us to reflect on the significance and meaning life. Even this ability to reflect is a gift. I believe that it is not our place to expect anything of God; this is where many

Expectations

people stray from the correct path. To expect something of God is to place you above Him and that is not a place where we belong.

I believe that life is to be lived. It's a vehicle that helps us to learn and to teach each other, and it is overall laborious in nature.

If there is anything to take away from these words it is probably this. Perhaps not everything is as it seems, perhaps it's not all about us, perhaps life, at times, is simply serving and teaching others. Perhaps we are meant to give as much as we take! We will feel more balanced and harmonious when we give to others.

Sadness is a time of reflection and an opportunity to see the many different possibilities that exist in life. Are you a victim, or are you just being handed more opportunities to learn, give and grow more spiritually complete? Are your latest woes a product of your own making?

What were your first thoughts when you woke up today? How might you have seen this day differently? Who were you laboring for today and what might be the purpose of your labor, in a bigger picture?

As I suggested earlier, unrealistic expectations cause many problems in our lives! Our expectations are often founded off of fantasy and wishful thinking and with even the smallest amount of thought and effort would, more often than not, be dispelled as unrealistic if we cared to consider them for a few moments. Care we should! All these unfulfilled expectations we have of life and others are the primary source of all of the pain we experience in life!

A Mind for Life

If we were to expect nothing of anyone, then everything good that happened would exceed our expectations. Smile! I know these words are maddening and perhaps even irritating. If you were to chew on them for awhile, however, you'd see how significant they are in regards to your life perspective and resulting disposition.

What is really hard when you are adopting a new mindset like this is accepting that even though you will expect nothing of others, everyone will still have expectations of you. Your reality and life will still be impacted by your ability to shape the perception of whether you are meeting or failing to meet all of these expectations.

I know you might have read this book looking for answers, and perhaps you may be disappointed that I've left you with so many questions. I believe though that your success will be defined by your own expectations and how you choose to view and act upon my words.

Yup, I really closed the chapter this way! Fittingly, I'm asking you not to expect so much of this chapter! Chuckle! Why did you expect anything different? How does it make you feel? Why do you feel that way? What does it mean to you? Smile!

Awareness develops from the questions you ask yourself and the analysis of your expectations!

Sometimes There Are No Shortcuts

Writing this book and developing a framework from my original life meanings and mixing the framework principles with passages of emotional reconciliation in order to help demonstrate that framework and provide you with real-life examples of it in action has been a fascinating journey for me.

It is in the same spirit that I share with you this next chapter. It's about experiencing and dealing with betrayal. I believe betrayal is one of the most difficult emotions we must face and handle. It can be equal and sometimes worse than experiencing the death of a loved one.

My reasoning for it being worse than loss is that often our betrayer continues to live and pop into our lives, generating a tremendous amount of negativity in us. Betrayal can cause us to feel powerful and dark emotions such as bewilderment, confusion, loss, anger, grief, hate and sadness. We may also banish our betrayer from our lives and, in that essence, they do die as they have become dead to us.

Because betrayal can only come after trust or high expectations it often blind sides us. We don't **EXPECT** it and it hits us like a freight train!

I experienced a huge betrayal some years ago. I won't get into it other than to say that most people might not see it as a big betrayal but I really struggled with it. The funny thing about betrayals is that they are very personal in nature. What can be an anthill to one person feels like Mount Everest to another. I tried to dismiss my feelings and told myself everyday that they were stupid.

Try as I might to ignore them, the hurt feelings inside me raged on like a burning inferno. Hence, the title of this chapter - sometimes you just can't cheat your emotions. Instead, you have to let go, experience the full brunt of your emotions and go through the inevitable healing process.

Another horrible thing about betrayal is that it leaves scars. Someone else can betray you in a small way and it's akin to them taking a knife and reopening wounds that never healed! Because of your past experience you feel more hurt when you are confronted with smaller betrayals in the future.

Since we are neck deep in these emotions, I'll share with you how I finally found healing. One day, out of the blue, I forgave those who

Sometimes There Are No Shortcuts

betrayed me. I started walking and talking with them everyday. I treated them a hundred times better than they treated me.

You see, I believe that forgiveness isn't really ours to give when someone hurts or betrays us. I believe that people have to find forgiveness within them when they do bad things to others. The more I forgave my betrayer, the more they reflected on their own actions. It was quite a journey for me, as normally I do just that, forgive and leave the burden with the aggressor to deal with. This betrayal, however, was so harsh that forgiveness eluded me for quite some time.

There was much confusion and bewilderment on my part because I just couldn't understand why I was betrayed and why people enjoyed kicking me when I was down. I ended up learning a lot about myself through this experience. I realized that I also had an ugly side and I had to deal with it. We often find our own ugliness in our fight to truly survive.

The reflection and introspection I experienced throughout this process was so large that it caused me to rethink my entire life. In the end, I changed everything and this book has poured forth in its wake. I'm certain that I'll never look at life the same way again.

Remember, forgiveness isn't your burden to carry. Forgive and move on because if you don't the aggressor will continue to hurt and betray you. It can become a spell that manifests into a death spiral of doom.

I do believe bad people have to live with themselves and that, karmically, they will pay for their actions over their lifetime. Many laugh at this notion, however my observations of bad people have led me to believe that they are usually perpetually unhappy. Their very nature doesn't allow them to be happy. They share misery instead of love.

With any betrayal we must ask ourselves if we were really betrayed by others or if we betrayed ourselves by expecting something or believing in something that wasn't real. Much of the hurt we experience in life is a result of our own actions or beliefs.

I am compelled to repeat this; much of our disappointment comes from our own ability to deceive ourselves. We believe in love, trust and a destiny that simply doesn't exist. We create an illusion to walk within and when the dream shatters we feel the ugliness of our failure. Betrayal is such a beast and mostly a result of our own naive illusions!

Because betrayal is often such a big event in our life, it can act like a portal or wormhole, leading to another dimension. That travel can lead us to a better place, or, more often, a worse place depending on how we choose to manage the situation. I know I was a quarter of the way down the time warp continuum headed to Badville when I had my revelation and jumped ship. I feel lucky to have jumped ship and drifted to a better place than I began.

If you've been betrayed, I hope that somewhere in my words you can see the same light I did and find your way to a better place. I hope that you can find a way to look at it all differently.

One of the things I love doing most is taking something bad and turning it into something really good. That is how I dealt with the betrayal I experienced and you can deal with your betrayal in the same way. If you aren't currently dealing with or recovering from a betrayal, perhaps this will help you in the future!

In the end, sometimes you need to let yourself break down, go through the cycle of emotions that come from your disappointment and then find your way forward. You'll know this is what you are experiencing when, try as you might, you can't find your way past what's bothering you. The simple acknowledgement that you can't beat it right now and that you just need time to heal can release a lot of pressure in itself. They say time heals all wounds and, while that logic is flawed when it comes to a fatal wound, there is a lot of healing power in the passing of time and in working through emotional disruptions, like those that come from betrayal and loss.

The reason this discussion is relevant is because A Mind For Life can teach you to expedite or shortcut many bad feelings and events in your life by helping you to look past the bad and find the good. Once mastered, this skill can be extremely useful and something you'll use almost daily. You may, as I did, become so accustomed to breezing through things that when something like a betrayal comes along it can really hurt you and your newfound skills will seem useless. Here again, the awareness that sometimes you can't sail through something will be what makes the difference in your eventual recovery.

Care And Respect

Sometimes it helps to take a sidebar to discuss various emotional aspects of our lives. Because of this, we'll focus on the concept of caring in this chapter.

When I first thought about the notion of caring, I was planning something very robust for this chapter; however, after careful consideration, I've elected to keep my thoughts on this subject focused and simple.

We appreciate and often expect others to care about us. We don't even think about whether we've earned their care and trust. Again, this is because we are so self-centered. For example, we expect lots of birthday gifts, yet we may give very few presents ourselves. You've surely heard the adage "you reap what you sew." I'll take this a bit further and say that you'll reap *some* of what you sew. This goes back to the fact that we expect too much in return for what we actually invest into others and life itself. Not every seed we plant yields dividends, some do not survive the elements!

People often fantasize about finding a person that wants nothing from them. The truth, however, is that anyone who lets you into their life in a significant way will want something from you. Whether it's friendship, love, respect, sympathy or one or more of a million other things, the truth is they want something from you, even if they don't consciously understand their expectations.

In life meanings I coined a concept that goes like this.

Sometimes we feel we don't get the respect we deserve. We value respect and often demand it even when we haven't earned it. We frequently wish to be treated better than we treat others. Respect, in my opinion, is governed by a simple formula: you probably only deserve a quarter of the respect you think you should have and you usually get back about a quarter of the respect you give out.

This formula also applies to caring.

I don't want to imply that in order to receive caring and respect you must give it. From a karmic standpoint that notion is all wrong, and it still implies some level of expectation. I talk a lot about reducing your expectations in this book and in many ways; I'd almost prefer that you give up expectations all together.

Of course reality dictates that we need to have some level of expectations in order to survive in this world and prevent others from taking advantage of us. I think it's more of an exercise in setting different levels of expectations. Expect, for instance, that when you go out to eat your order will be messed up and you will have to correct it in some way. If you go into situations with that level of expectation, you won't get as uptight and tense when things do go wrong and you'll feel better when things go right.

Let's get back to the ideas of caring and respect! Some people are naturally caring while others are much more focused on themselves. Naturally caring people tend to get upset with those who aren't as nurturing. If you aren't a naturally caring person, you probably don't understand this or even care much about it. You also probably don't understand that this impacts how you are perceived and, ultimately, the direction your life takes. Some people think it's stupid to care about and give to others; they simply take and take without any reciprocation.

My experiences have led me to believe that a person's level of caring has a lot to do with their level of self-balance and happiness. One of the strange truths in life is that you can't find happiness if you can't care about and be happy for others.

This notion is an unspoken rule and a common element to the great expectations framework. I have to laugh when I tell you this; however, in my humble opinion, the reality of human psychology is that, without expectations, society as we know it would collapse. Rest assured though that I'm not asking you to forgo your expectations and destroy society!

I believe that every input has an output and that every action has a reaction. If we attempted to mathematically develop a formula for life it would certainly encompass these principals.

Assessing how caring you are is a great exercise to undertake. Below is a scale and guidelines against which you can measure yourself; ten is the highest score. I don't believe, however, that it's a good idea to be a ten; I'll explain why later.

ZERO: You go out of your way to make life difficult for others and, perversely, you enjoy seeing them struggle!

1. You don't really think about helping or doing anything for anyone else.
2. Occasionally, you think maybe you should help or care.
3. You sometimes feel a little remorse or guilt for how little you care for others.
4. You'll lend a hand when asked.
5. You sometimes think to help or care without being asked.
6. You believe you shouldn't make yourself a burden on others and help and care accordingly.
7. You help others frequently.
8. You help others all of the time!
9. You put others before yourself almost all of the time.
10. You care for and give to others without regard to yourself.

It's not a perfect scale; it's just meant to stimulate thought. Take some time, be honest with yourself and determine where you fall on the scale.

The next exercise is to list reasons why caring might be important to you. Some examples might be as follows:

- Caring for others makes me feel good.
- Caring for others ensures that others will care for me.
- I like the way others smile when I care for them.
- I believe everyone should care for someone.
- My caring saves lives.

Care And Respect

- Caring is important in my spiritual beliefs.
- Caring allows me to feel good about looking myself in the mirror when I wake up each day.
- I find the more I care for others, the more they care for me and that makes me smile, be happy and feel good.

Some of your reasons may be shrewder; it simply depends on how you're wired. A couple of examples of these more devious reasons are:

- It's important to me that I be perceived as a caring person.
- I stand to lose things if I don't show I care about others.

After you've made this list, you should determine where on the scale you would like to be. If there is a gap between where you are and where you want to be, decide how you can close it. You can develop your own set of actions that you think will help you get or reach your goal, or you can attach yourself to an appropriate model, as we've previously discussed.

The key to changing yourself is to be continually aware (develop and read your notes regularly) and to live the positive postures you created using your notes.

Finding the right way to care about others is also important. Some techniques will effectively work for you while other methods will not.

If caring for others isn't making you feel better about yourself then you need to call a time out in order to reassess your notes and then start over with a new plan. Don't forget to care about yourself. If you spend all of your energy and effort caring about others with no regard for yourself, you'll become drained and be of no use to anyone.

Only you can decide how much caring means to you and how it impacts your own life. Looking in the mirror can truly be difficult. By nature, most people are more designed to be selfish and uncaring. Sometimes I've even wondered if this attitude is a development issue. We are born into the world and, right from the very start, it's me, me, me!

It's funny how we depend on others to care for us and help us to develop but we lean towards caring for no one until perhaps we have children. Even then, some people return to their original nature and do just enough for their children to keep themselves out of jail. It's really quite sad when you think about it.

Developing your sense and awareness of caring is an essential part of developing A Mind For Life.

Pain And Sorrow

Many of us hold on to and continually polish our pain and sorrow without even realizing it! It becomes our personal identifying crest and the centerpiece of our life.

The signs are easily visible to others and are often the results of a betrayal or loss. When it's betrayal, we find ourselves lamenting about the person who betrayed us years beyond the conclusion of the relationship. Perhaps our betrayer continues to taunt and hurt us as well, making it seemingly impossible to walk away.

Sorrow stems from loss and feelings of incompleteness or unfinished business. Perhaps you lost someone you were in the middle of falling in love with and your feelings were at their peak. Loss of this sort is not easy to deal with. Maybe you lost a person who was a longtime fixture in your life, and you simply miss them. If the person you lost was a confidant, the loss is even more difficult, since you may feel like you lost the only person who understood you.

The pain and loss can become immense! How do we get to a point where we can move on?

Let's begin with discussing how to deal with betrayal. I suggest you compare betrayal to a cancer that must be removed and cast away. Symbolically, we need to cut it from ourselves, put it in a lead container, tie a rock to it and throw it in the deepest lake we can find. While this is not physically possible, it is a great symbolic exercise. (See **Sometimes there are no Shortcuts** for more on dealing with betrayal.)

Practically speaking, we must understand that we enable and energize those who've hurt us by dwelling on the pain they caused. Like soldiers returning home from the battlefield, we must deny the images of war that rage in our own head, in order to become productive citizens.

In part, we must reprogram these hurts to a neutral registry in our brain. We move it from one painful container in our brain to another neutral, historical container. Another great place to move these hurts is to the "Lessons Learned Shelf," the "Changed My Life Pallet" or the "I'm Grateful and Better Off Shelf."

Our memories and life experiences reside in a virtual life warehouse. Much of the art of reprogramming is learning to move and rearrange our memories within that warehouse. Perhaps you can liken it to moving hazardous waste from a leaking barrel on the top shelf to a safe, concrete disposal unit on the ground floor in back of the warehouse. It's less likely to hurt and bother us there.

Pain And Sorrow

If we can take the hurt and move it to a positive turning point in our lives, the result will be even better!

Loss is tremendously difficult. The idea of transforming loss may seem unimaginable, but it is doable. You simply have to find a way to move the loss from the "Hurt File" to the "Great Memories File" or the "Source of Inspiration File." Perhaps the person you lost will live on inside of you as a voice that helps you when you are in times of trouble. Perhaps this is how people truly experience life after death, as an energy and spirit that lives on in others. My grandfather lives on inside me. It's a powerful place for the person you lost and a great feeling that will make you smile when you realize you've found the rightful place for the one you loved, trusted and valued so much in your life.

Developing a full awareness about what is troubling you and exploring it until you find answers is one of the keys to moving forward. Furthermore, you must occasionally acknowledge that there are no answers to be had. I've moved things to the holding space in my warehouse many times. Later, I often find the enlightenment and wisdom to deal with them that I didn't originally have. Of course, sometimes when you look in the holding space you find, like you do in your basement, that you no longer care about the things you have there and are able to simply pitch them.

Sometimes, time itself is the answer!

Enemy Number One

As I've stated before, much of what we've learned over the course of our life is a lie that has been passed to us by our forbearers or major influencers of our own time.

What I haven't really talked about is the web of lies we weave for ourselves. We love to weave a web where we seem nearly perfect. We regularly lie to ourselves in order to justify our mistakes, fill-in the gaps of our own failures and, in general, prop ourselves up. These self-made lies are essential to our own esteem and ability to keep forging through life.

When we get called out on our lies and failure stares us in the face, we experience turmoil and dismay. The rose-colored mirror we've created and been staring into suddenly cracks, and our self-view becomes shattered, confusing and even ugly.

Talking about and dealing with this subject is a little like playing with nitroglycerin; it's a very unstable and dicey business. We're all like this – most of us have unrealistic views of ourselves.

Not to go all Twilight Zone on you, but you may liken this phenomenon to one where we live and exist in multiple dimensions. Are you scratching your head right now, wondering what in the world I am talking about?

Think of it like this. There is your own view of yourself and then there is the way you appear to every other person in this world. You might think that those who we are closest to us will see us in our truest form. This is debatable, however, since the people closest to us are often part of the alter egos we weave. We lose objectivity when we become fond of someone and are much quicker to look past their shortcomings. If we polled the ten people who interacted with you most we would get varying opinions and views as to how you actually are. Imagine you're watching those closest to you get together and talk about you after your funeral. Wouldn't each be able to surprise the others with some aspect of you they never knew or experienced? Whose view of you is correct?

If we were to sort through and find the truth of it, the realistic you is only partially how you see yourself. How others see and perceive you is a reality unto its own; these perceptions greatly impact your existence. They determine, in part, what kind of living you make, how you are treated, how much love you have and how much trouble you have.

How we see ourselves impacts how others see us, and how others see us impacts our lives. This can be a loop if we aren't careful.

Enemy Number One

Seeing ourselves poorly causes others to see us poorly which, in turn, causes us to feel more poorly about ourselves. It's not difficult to see how this sort of logic can spiral out of control, is it? Nonetheless, it's worth noting that sometimes others see us better than we see ourselves. If you are extremely self-centered, you will have a higher opinion of yourself than others do. Conversely, if you're kind and humble others will likely perceive you to be better than you see yourself.

Our own reflection upon our life and experiences influence how we see ourselves; we travel in a sort of circle. Let's say life, in part, is measured by how far we get from the center of the circle. When we travel in a circle, we never gain any distance from its center. Instead, we must make choices that allow us to escape the centrifugal force of the circle. Our awareness impacts our ability to make some of these choices. If we stop and think about our choices before we make them, however, we can change the circle, flatten it into a straight line and actually ride the line to get further from the original center.

The fact that anyone who interacts with you wants something is not completely bad. It's part of our core makeup to need to be needed. You see, even when we give, that giving is often about fulfilling our own desire to be needed or liked. We also desire to be seen as kind, smart, humble and, of course, beautiful.

The real reason I bring this all up is to show you that you must step away from yourself a bit in order to gain a more realistic view of who you are. Having that grounded view of yourself is very helpful if you make use of it. Just don't take it too far and try to become someone you aren't. You might be thinking that this whole book is, in essence, about changing yourself and who you are. I suggest that when you make changes you stop and think carefully about why you are making them and whether they are leading you towards or away from the real you and who you want to be in the future. Don't attempt to change if you don't embrace and desire the changes you're attempting to make.

Something else to consider is this, whose view of you matters? Is it your view of yourself that matters most to you, or is it everyone else's? For many, this questions is not as obvious to those who believe it's truly their own view that matters. There's the Twilight Zone music again! Reality is truly warped and dependent on whose eye's your looking through!

The fact that we can suppress some of our more undesirable emotions doesn't mean we'll get rid of them all together. In order to maintain balance, we need some of the bad. Consider the desire for power, for example. If you try not to seek out and desire power, you'll still likely have enough of the residue of the natural desire for power in order to maintain a healthy balance.

Take time and think about why you are your own worst enemy. There is more to come that will help you continue to explore this notion. If you haven't gained awareness of it yet, keep going. The next chapters are all building towards something bigger!

Look back! Wow! The distance is growing behind you! Turn your focus ahead! Your destination draws closer!

Alberta Falls
Mark Abraham
Rocky Mountain National Park 2005

Resting and relaxing, halfway to the bottom of the return trail. The sounds and views are calming to the soul and heart. There is time to sip some water and contemplate our life's reflections as we take in the wonders of nature and of our existence in general.

Why Do We Hate So Much!

One day I started thinking about why people dislike each other. Where does the dislike come from? As an observer of people, I see it all the time. Sometimes people admit they have no good reason for their feelings. They say, "I don't know why, but I do not like that person! That person is ugly! That person is dumb! I get a bad feeling about that person." The list goes on and on.

How do we come to dislike people we barely know or don't know at all? I think some of it comes from our failure to accept people who don't fit our preconceived expectations. The capacity to dislike others is often our own fault, not the fault of others. It's an ugly side of the human spirit that we see and experience every day of our lives. No matter who you are, there are people who will irrationally dislike you. In their opinion, you're too sweet, too good looking, not smart enough or maybe you just part your hair the wrong way.

All of it this stems from the enemy within. We collect and project feelings of hate through our behavior and actions. Some might say its karma; however, I believe it's more about how some of us are programmed and wired. We may be genetically predisposed to certain attitudes and demeanors. Currently, there is a lot of research into genetics and, as science progresses, we'll come to learn more and more about its effects. The rest of our attitudes are created from using our environment, training and, of course, ourselves.

When we're young, we learn from our parents and other adults in our lives. We also learn from TV and it often paints unrealistic worlds for us to escape to where the actors have limited consequences for their actions. If you doubt me then, simply ask people you know why they watch and like TV so much. Everything is better on TV than it is in reality - it's truly an escape for many of us. If people on TV mirrored reality, they would be struggling and living uninteresting lives and there is little entertainment value in that!. Just imagine what people could accomplish if they took the time they spend watching TV and invested it elsewhere. Reality TV, why is it so unreal? Smile! Don't get me wrong, I'm guilty of it myself.

Enough about TV, let's get back to our exploration of our ugly side. What am I trying to get at with this? I'm trying to get you to ask yourself why you have these feelings towards other people. Why do you feel the need to remark or think about how another person looks? Why don't we simply focus on ourselves and how we look, speak, walk, dress and act?

Why Do We Hate So Much!

Why aren't we more passive about others when they don't even interact with us? In part, it's due to the natural human instinct to compare ourselves to each other. I had to laugh the other day when one of the young ladies in my life asked me why ugly girls had boyfriends and she didn't. I told her that there was more to being a beautiful person than looks. My advice, however, fell upon deaf ears, as is the case with many of today's youth.

When we criticize others, it's more a criticism of ourselves than it is of them. Think about it for a minute. We have to allow others to change, and see that change, or no one will ever be able to actually change for us.

When you're critical of others you're unconsciously saying that you wouldn't like to look, act, dress, speak or behave the way that person does. It can't really be anything else if you don't know and aren't interacting with the person you are criticizing. I see it all the time, for instance, when people watch TV and comment about the actors.

I stated earlier that the world does not really change all that much, it is us, ourselves, that change the most. We are all constantly evolving, growing and changing. Because we are so self-centered though, we often fail to see how others evolve. When we do see those changes, consciously they do not register and unconsciously we often respond with agitation or resistance to the changes the people closest to us make. Even when those changes are very positive ones, our unconscious blocks it out and we often refuse to see the new side of people. It takes awareness and lots of questioning of ourselves to break that cycle and to see people for who they become. Both the good and the bad!

A Mind for Life

When feeling challenged, you can go through the questioning exercises I have shared with you in this book. Why do I care? How does it impact me? Is it worth my time and energy? Most times you'll realize you do not care. I guess if a person takes this logic too far you could question whether or not you should simply brush off your own existence. The rule I suggest is that you want to apply this to negative emotions. When you sense your pulse is accelerating and your level of agitation or frustration is increasing, call a timeout and ask yourself why you are feeling this way.

This technique really works and can result in a greater level of happiness. If you're not experiencing a negative emotion then you are either in the neutral zone or on the happy side of the scale. I find that remaining passive to people who don't impact my life really does have value. If you play with this notion a bit, I believe you'll value it as well, and you'll also begin to feel better about yourself.

When you're tearing down others you are, in essence, also tearing down yourself. Even though our adaptive nature prompts us to lie to ourselves, negative emotions are lurking in the shadows of our unconscious. They build up over time and impact our self-worth.

Dare yourself not to compare! The next time you run across someone you don't like, ask yourself what you do like about them and then try building upon that thought!

Diversity

While a large part of society focuses on diversity as a workplace topic, I believe it has great significance in our personal lives and in our development of greater awareness.

Someone long ago asked me how I came to have so much awareness; I had no response. I literally said "I don't know." Recently, I began to think about that question again and I realized I probably did have at least a partial answer.

I think a great deal of my awareness is the result of my life experience. I grew up in a very nice upper-middleclass home. Then, my parents divorced and many things changed. I still had all the basics; however, there were many kids in school that had things I didn't. I'm not complaining about what I didn't have. In fact, I now believe that it was a good thing that taught me to appreciate and value the things parents do provide for us.

A Mind for Life

Needless to say we all feel a certain kind of awkwardness at times when we see other people that live in different socioeconomic classes. We are aware of who has more than us and all of the things that we don't have. This is our material programming at work.

I moved to New York to live with my father and go to boarding school when I was about thirteen. Living on my own in a new and strange place, I began to become very aware of the people and places surrounding me,

When I was seventeen. I graduated from high school early and joined the Army. I endured more strange places and environments as I went through boot camp, occupational training and then to my first assignment. At eighteen, I was sent to the conflict in Grenada and then I was assigned to a base in Italy when I was nineteen.

Living in another country and then traveling to even more countries as a part of my duties in the Army fostered more and more awareness in me. In a foreign country, you become the foreigner and are treated as such. There were both good and bad aspects to living this way. I started a bar business in Italy and encountered even more diverse people. I also taught English to Italians for a commercial school. Then I worked back at the military base in a department store unloading trucks and stocking shelves.

Finally, at age twenty-six, I moved back to the Unites States and tried to develop a career. I went back to school, got a degree and set off into the white collar working world of which I am part of today.

Diversity

The point of my story is that we can inherit awareness through our life experiences and by embracing diversity. Many times what constitutes unthinkable change becomes a lesson in adaptation. Very seldom, in all those jobs and places, did I ever feel out of place or unwelcome.

Talking to and living with other people of different nationalities, cultures, languages and mindsets make us more aware of our own programming. We realize that people in different countries do things differently from us, and they still survive and thrive. Their approach often runs against our own programming and understanding of how things work and should be. It's funny because, in a way, you can almost think of it as a parallel dimension where people do things differently and yet go on living, perfectly fine.

The arrogance of our youth causes us to question why other cultures do things the wrong way, but the wisdom of our middle and later years increases our appreciation of diversity. Being submerged in a diverse world gives us an appreciation that is truly humbling. Extremists lack the rewards diversity offers and, therefore, fear it.

I don't believe we see and feel all of this when we limit our exposure to the confines of our own tiny islands. Change is scary and so is facing diversity. However, as I've said elsewhere in this book, learning to embrace change is exciting and also highly rewarding.

One of the ways you can increase your personal and social self-awareness is to explore outside your own island. Embrace some diversity and see how it feels. You don't have to like it to benefit from it. Try not to judge - remember that the people you are judging could easily sit in judgment of you as well.

A Mind for Life

If you don't want to be judged and condemned as you judge and condemn others then you'll need to be open minded and tolerant of others who are different than you.

If you look back over your shoulder, you'll see the mountains to your rear growing smaller; you've made significant progress. The belief that you'll complete the journey grows stronger!

Teton Sunset

Mark Abraham
Grand Tetons 2006

The frost glazed the fields and the tips of my fingers as I waited for the sun to light the mountain tops with its fiery red glow. Even the spirit of the bitter cold yields to the optimism the dawn of a new day brings and its master, our sun!

All About Power

So many people seem to desire power. They want money, fame and the ability to direct their lives and control others. Given that desire, I suppose this chapter may be disturbing to a few people.

Power is very alluring; it's one of the fundamental things we all seek to obtain at some point in our lives. The desire to be powerful often surfaces when we are children; we get tired of being pushed around and dreaming of the day when we will rule the world. Other times the desire develops later in life and people get consumed with wielding power over others. It might even be triggered by feelings of revenge towards someone who has hurt you. People desire and seek to gain power over others and sometimes do questionable things to obtain it.

True power is the ability to have control over our own minds and selves and to feel void of the need to wield power over others.

A Mind for Life

Sometimes people enjoy wielding their power try to capture us in their web of control. In my career, I've run across many people who seem to thrive off humiliating others. They push and shove until they see their target wilt and crumble. This makes them feel big, excited and powerful. To people like this, it's not about right or wrong or even getting something accomplished. Instead, they see their power as a toy and a way to achieve an adrenalin rush. It's a cycle of self-actualization they repeat over and over again.

I can't explain why some people are wired this way. There is probably someone reading this book right now who is predisposed to this behavior. Unfortunately, people like this will probably be oblivious to my words. It goes back to our inherent ability to see ourselves as angels. Power seekers steal energy from the meek; they build themselves up at the expense of others. A power seeker will often go crazy if someone even questions their power or ability to control others. Their instinct is to go out and squash someone in order to prove their might.

Ironically, people outside the victim/perpetrator circle tend to see these power perpetrators as pathetic and weak minded people. Outsiders are able to see that the so-called powerful people lack self-control and humility and are too full of self-importance. It's the exact opposite image that a power seeker desires; they want to appear strong, authoritative and in control. If you are a power seeker, a key reprogramming tool is to tell yourself that your need for power is weak and pathetic. This will help you reprogram and live more effectively as you redirect your energy towards self-improvement and achieving greater harmony with those around you.

There are many ways to deal with people who thrive on power. What they seem to seek most is a reaction from others. They need this reaction in order to confirm their power; if you don't react, then they won't get the validation they are seeking and their power will not become actualized. Passive power seekers like to cause a disruption and reaction but hide in the shadows as not to experience the fallout or consequences of their actions. Absolute power seekers have an almost bullish and confrontational nature; experiencing the reaction at ground zero is too exciting for them to resist.

If a person like this attempts to bother or provoke you, then you can take their power away by failing to react and demonstrating they have no effect on you.

These people's egos, however, will often drive them to continue to attempt to control you. In some cases, this can be a very dangerous and even deadly game. If continually denied dominion over you, they may become more and more agitated and violent as they escalate their actions against you in order to solicit the response they crave. This is often illustrated in news stories about people committing unthinkable acts. They can get so wrapped up in their quest for power that they lose what little common sense they have left and push things over the edge of sanity. Lead a power seeker to a cliff for their actualization and often they'll jump right off it if they believe power is within their reach. This is because they lack self-control and have very inflated egos.

Show up an egomaniac and you may have an enemy for life. It's often difficult to determine how you should handle a power seeker. If it's of no cost and consequence to you, it may be best to simply toss them a token bone in order to get yourself off their radar. Don't let them know you've outsmarted them, however, or they'll be right back to square one with an enraged ego.

Other times the only way to stop a power seeker from bullying you or others is to get in their face and scare them. If you are too difficult or painful for them to deal with then they will find somewhere else to get their fix. Many of these people lack courage, which is why they behave in the way they do. Power seekers posses a very odd set of character attributes. Sometimes simple confrontation is all it takes. In the jungle two grand lions may respect each other and be mindful of the destruction each can wield upon the other. In these cases of mutually assured destruction, the lions simply mark off their own territory and protect their stake in the world.

There are also more virulent ways of dealing with these power hungry people. Often dealing with power seekers in a passive manner leads them right into a trap of their own making. The egomaniac willingly walks themselves right into it because of their wiring and blindness to their own weaknesses. It's like the mouse eating the tainted cheese; it simply can't help itself! If you lay the right breadcrumb trail an egomaniac will follow it; they are very susceptible to hanging themselves. The same goes for greedy people. Con artists play on people's greed and fear all the time. Most egomaniacs are very easy to trap and, more often than not, will find their own demise without any intervention from you.

Finally, getting a power seeker to believe they are weak because they seek power and control over others can create a self-obsessive loop. They'll feel compelled to hold back in order to demonstrate that they really do have power! I know your probably laughing right now, but this might be the ultimate way to deal with a power seeker. Take a power seeker by the hand and see if you can get them to see the error of their ways. Just like the story of the thorn being removed from the beasts paw, you may find a friend for life.

All About Power

I've talked enough about the bad side of power, now let's explore its good side. Real power is doing good, making smiles and bringing warmth to what is often a cold world. By using our skills, leadership, courage, faith and ability to bring people together, we can find good power. Real power lies in our ability to effectively influence others towards the goal of common good, without any need for recognition.

You can thrive off of this sort of power. Nevertheless, there is still a problem with needing any kind of power. Even people who use their power with good intentions are, at heart, still addicted to power. If this sort of reprogramming helps to bring about more good; however, it's certainly a step in the right direction.

Questioning yourself about a craving or addiction is a great way to get more clarity on the subject. I want you to stop and think for a minute about questioning the need for power. It's important to note that power seekers often crave attention and, in part, this is the allure of exerting their power over others.

What does becoming powerful cost us, not financially, but spiritually? Will it cost you trust and respect in the eyes of others? We've talked about respect elsewhere in A Mind For Life– in this instance I am referring to positive respect, not fear-based respect.

Since power seekers are usually very self-centered and have little care or concern for others, they often have no idea that people view them poorly. This is why self-centeredness is truly a weakness; it leaves us blind and ultimately rejected by others.

How does seeking power complicate my life? Do I find myself having to juggle all kinds of tasks and people in order to actualize my power? Is all the time I spend accumulating power worth it? What else could I be doing with my time?

Does my power bring about good, or does it come at the expense of others? Do I feel good about my power when I look in the mirror? Will I have regrets later?

How do seemingly powerless people create so much change and good in the world? How do they do so with no need for recognition?

This questioning and exploration of yourself and your motives will be both frustrating and rewarding. If you can't see past a material existence into a spiritual life, you may even get depressed; life may seem empty without all the material things you are accustomed to. Maybe that's my final point and question. Do we really need to be powerful if we detach ourselves from a material existence?

Celebrating Quietly

When life is going well we often want to stand on the mountaintop and proclaim our success to everyone. I want to take a few moments to try and talk you down from the mountain. By reflecting on my grandfather's life, I've learned that there may be more happiness in quiet localized celebrations than there is center stage at the Hollywood Bowl.

As we discuss this topic, we should further explore the notion of success. As you've probably already gathered, I believe success is happiness. Furthermore, I feel that happiness is based on the spiritual aspects of life and not the material ones. Current research even indicates that people at higher income levels seem to be happier because of the type of job they have rather than any financial benefits they reap.

A Mind for Life

My grandfather was a modest man. He, like many of our parents, worked hard, brought home a modest paycheck, provided for his family and lived modestly. He was a quiet man; he could be very wise if engaged in conversation; and fully understood the merits of living a simple life. He was happy, for the most part, and he never had a need to broadcast his happiness. He quietly enjoyed his simple life and celebrated by sharing his love and wisdom of life with others.

When we celebrate out loud we often get lots of attention. We feel as if everyone should join in and tout the greatness of our accomplishments and success. We get disappointed and often judgmental when others fail to jump on our bandwagon. We get even more dismayed when others cast stones at us and try to knock us off our wagon. Simply stated, we get more attention than we want and or that is good for us. When others view our success as their own failure, we get even more unwanted attention.

If more of us realized that touting our own successes makes others feel bad, our celebrations might be far more reserved. Those who are self centered and insensitive, however, probably wouldn't be swayed by this knowledge. Instead, they would simply say others shouldn't poop on their parade!

The point I'm trying to make is that there is tremendous poise and benefit to being able to celebrate more quietly. The ability to rid ourselves of our in-your-face attitude and need for attention will mark a major victory in our life. Getting to this point may be very difficult for some, as it's contrary to their true nature.

Sharing our successes with those closest to us surrounds us with a calm, warm feeling; savoring the simplicity of the moment will

Celebrating Quietly

certainly bring a smile to our lips. As for all that attention you once craved, you'll probably realize it just makes life more complicated and that you're better off keeping it more low key!

Emotional Efficiency

The ultimate formula for navigating life successfully is probably about 30% focus on yourself and 70% focus on your duties and on others. The actual percentages aren't nearly as important as the thought behind them.

If we focus too much on ourselves then, relatively speaking, some of the things we need to do go undone. I'll elaborate on this concept later. If we focus too much on our duties and on others then our spirit will become weighted and we'll grow de-energized.

In an ideal world, we'd be able to take care of our duties and also ourselves. It might sound impossible; however, if we break it down it will become easier to see how to put theory into practice.

Our physical body is a duty; we are obligated to take care of it or it will deteriorate and experience failures.

A Mind for Life

When many people think of exercise they think of a gym, a lot of hard, hard work and tons of sweat. What I'd like you to consider is that perhaps hard work like that is extreme; all you really need to do is mix up some moderate exercise and activity throughout your week and maintain a reasonable diet.

As I've said before, much of what we feel is self-imposed and created. If you view a walk at lunch as exercise then it may seem like a burden. If you believe walking isn't real exercise, you might take the walk for enjoyment in the morning or for lunch and then do some other sport or workout in the evening. Perspective is golden in its ability to shape our lives.

If we don't perform our duties we get behind – just like if we neglect our bodies we become overweight. When we become overweight, we must exert more effort in order to become fit again. In order to remove the excess weight, we often begin a vigorous workout schedule. The burden of this schedule then becomes too much, leading us back to our old habits and we find ourselves in the middle of a potentially damaging cycle.

This is illustrative of the paradox of self and duty. We fail to focus on our duties, then we get behind, and we can get so far behind that we can actually trap ourselves. Freeing ourselves requires extraordinary effort. The prospect of extraordinary effort often breaks our spirit down and we fail to meet the challenge. Psychologically, it becomes too difficult!

This is why maintaining a balance between self and duty is beneficial in both the short-term and long-term. The benefits and failures are cumulative in nature.

Emotional Efficiency

The hidden impact of the failure to maintain this balance is that it creates an emotional roller coaster consisting of peaks of self-focused highs and valleys of **deep** holes we have to climb out of for neglecting our duties.

If we keep active and eat right, health problems will, most likely, not be a challenge we have to face.

In an ideal state, we'd enjoy activities like walks, bike rides, tennis and jogging. In a perfect world, we'd enjoy healthy food and be satisfied with healthy portions. If we did these things, we'd achieve health harmony.

While I picked health as an example, the same formula applies to almost every aspect of our life: relationships, careers, futures, retirement, etc. The more harmony we bring to each facet of life, the easier life gets. Coincidently, I think you'll also find the more you simplify your life the easier it becomes to achieve harmony.

Those of you who are scientifically oriented might object to this theory. Some of you may think that completely harmonious lives are bound to be incredibly boring and uneventful. Drama kings and queens thrive on drama; they create drama and then, when it gets to be too much, want to escape. Just remember that drama is highly overrated and you'll be okay. Smile! The need for drama is an addiction and should be treated that way.

I understand that life without mansions, exciting cars, tons of diamonds and caviar chased with champagne may seem mundane. But I'd have you consider a few things in response to these objections. Furthermore, the more expectations we have, the less likely we are to experience happiness. In fact, expectations and happiness are often inversely proportionate to each other!

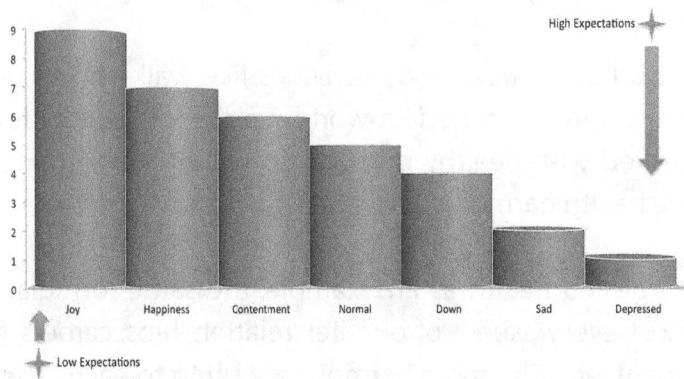

Questions we should ask are as follows.

- Why do we equate happiness with material possession and particular life styles?
- When you have good stuff all the time doesn't it become average and then mundane?
- If you believe all those material objects are the spice of life, do you not become potentially enslaved to a means of obtaining and interacting with them?
- If you end up enslaved, don't you ultimately begin to desire freedom?
- Isn't the ideal state, therefore, to minimize lows, experience and enjoy the highs and feel more relaxed and happy?

How is all this not one giant conflict?

Emotional Efficiency

It's a complex notion to understand, and I'm hoping you'll benefit from the years of thought I've already put into it.

I've told you in the past that you have to experience lows in order to appreciate highs. If you can unconditionally accept the lows and be grateful for the highs then you can begin to find the sort of harmony I have described.

It's human nature to get cocky and bask in the highs and forget about the lows. This, however, usually ends with us crashing down and hitting a real low point.

If you expect lows and remain fearful and pensive about them, then their impact is lessened. This perspective also allows you to gratefully appreciate the highs and to reach a sweeter spot when you experience them.

Life, of course, isn't always meant to be fun. Instead, it's all about achieving an overall balance. If you see life as 90% bad and 10% good, then simply seeing life 10% better will double your happiness. If you could simply achieve a 50/50 balance, your life would seem unimaginably better.

Another principle I'd like to discuss is called thinking between the twenties. This principle involves not thinking too much to the left or too much to the right! The truth lies somewhere in between the two extremes and is often very different than we expect it to be. Sometimes we look for answers in the wrong direction and the truth ends up being something completely different than we expected.

For example, we may think that we have to align ourselves to extreme political views. Political views on major polarizing issues tend to be within the extreme far left or the extreme far right. This equates, on our scale, to thinking between the twenties: the left being 1-20 and the right 80-100. We can get caught up in these extremes and forget all the thoughts that exist between 20 and 80. This middle zone represents a greater amount of possibilities and, most likely, contains the best choice. That's why they're called polarizing issues – they attempt to pull people to the extremes. We must remember that we don't have to choose extremes. In fact, I sincerely believe people who choose to think between the 20's find their lives a lot more palatable.

Another thought process that goes hand in hand with thinking between the twenties is the notion that we often chase the wrong goals. Many people, for instance, think that finding the right person to share their life with will complete them. Literally, people believe it's the answer to the remainder of their unhappiness. They search and search for what they believe is the holy grail of life: the perfect soul mate.

Ironically, this dogged pursuit of a soul mate often causes us a lot of unhappiness. It's very hard to find that person and, more often than not, you'll find them when you aren't actively looking. To be honest, it's also naïve to believe that finding the right partner will solve all your problems. You can find your soul mate and have a great companion but still live in hell on earth. Still, our expectations of finding the perfect soul mate and the happiness they will give us are extreme – we're still not thinking between the twenties. No other person, not even your soul mate, can complete you. We must complete ourselves. Furthermore, we must be complete in order to positively interact with our soul mate; if we aren't, we run the risk of bringing them down with us. One last thought, do you really expect some person to become the answer to all your problems? Aren't you setting them up for failure before you ever meet them?

Avoid extremes if you can, and make sure you keep your eyes open to the possibility that things aren't always as they seem and that the goals you're chasing may not be the right answer to life. Many rich people, for example, have more problems and experience greater unhappiness than poor people who are content to live simple lives geared more towards spirituality. To some degree, we are comforted by allowing the current of life to carry us away. Just remember that you can't totally let go! If you find yourself floating with the current, remember to wear a life jacket and take other protective measures against the harsh rapids which may lie ahead.

I can remember driving to work and feeling hurried and tense and dreading the day ahead. These days my drive is a more pleasant experience; I look at the sun, trees, or even rain, listen to music and have a nice time. I still work in what many consider a high stress job. The difference is my attitude; I've learned to not let so many things bother me and rule my life. Instead, I focus my energy on solving the things that will cause me pain if I don't take care of them.

Many stereotypically successful people take care of business first and themselves second. I think this is a great approach, so long as we don't allow the amount of business we have to take care of rule and take over our life. Again, it's necessary and right to invest in ourselves.

A Mind for Life

When we take care of the others, meet our commitments, live up to our word and fulfill our promises; we feel and live better. People respect us more and treat us better. That's why it's important to keep life simple and not make more promises than we can realistically honor. We must also make sure that people don't mistake our intentions for promises.

The notion of emotional efficiency is definitely worth considering. It's key to achieving a better and simpler life! In short, don't make your life more complicated than it needs to be and you'll be rewarded with more time and freedom.

Expectations Be Darned!

I've been relentless in my efforts to get you to rethink how much you should expect from life. Let's assume for a moment I have failed. Maybe I can't get you to see it differently. Suppose I concede to that it's okay for you to have expectations and I let you continue to build new ones.

If you are going to continue forming expectations, you should at least adopt a method that allows you to make realistic ones. If I can't convince you that setting unrealistic expectations will lead to disappointments then I simply can't help you!

So, how do we go about making realistic expectations? Let's explore!

A Mind for Life

When creating an expectation we should ask ourselves several questions in order to ascertain how realistic the expectation is and the likelihood that it will be met.

Suppose you have an expectation that your hard work this year should result in a vacation to a tropical island. You can use any example you want, but for illustrative purposes, let's stick with this one for starters.

In your mind perhaps you are saying to yourself the following. I've worked a lot of overtime this year and will have a nice bonus to stash away. I've saved up vacation days and believe I will have the time and money to go somewhere nice! It'll be December and so a tropical island, fruity drinks, a tan all look like great rewards for my hard work. An expectation is born!

Since you've read this book and gained awareness an AM4L alarm will probably go off in your head at this point! You'll say to yourself, "Stop!" "Timeout here!"

Your mind will become flooded with a variety of questions. Have you ever managed to actually save money for a vacation in the past? How realistic is it that the money you need will really be there when the end of the year arrives? Are there Christmas gifts to purchase or other year end expenses to consider? The point of these questions is to ascertain how likely it is that you'll really be able to save the money?

Then other questions will start swirling around in your brain. How likely is it that a year end project will to come up at the office and prohibit you from taking time off? When will the vacation actually

Expectations Be Darned!

fit into your family schedule? Will everyone else be able to go? Historically, what usually happens at that time of year?

So you've asked a few questions now, and depending on who you are and how things have played out historically you may have a better foundation for your expectations. Either you'll scale your expectations back, create a robust plan to make sure they become real, or feel good about them as they sit.

X Factor	3	2	3	1	1
Entry	5	2	2	5	5
	Historical	Variables	Commitment	Planning	Time
Scale	What is the historical track record for you and success as it relates to this expectation	How many People or other dependencies or single points of failure is related to your expecation	What is the level of overall commitments to the expectation for all parties and dependencies?	How well has the plans been made and reviewed	How much time for the expectation to be met?
10	Never Happens	10 or more points of failure	No Commitment	No real plan	No time
9	10% of time success	9 points of failure	10% Commitment	plans in my head	Very little time
8	20% of time success	8 points of failure	20% Commitment	plan is on TP	little time
7	30% of time success	7 points of failure	30% Commitment	loosely planned	Some time
6	40% of time success	6 points of failure	40% Commitment	Planned no review	less than average time
5	50% of time success	5 points of failure	50% Commitment	Well planned no review	Average time
4	60% of time success	4 points of failure	60% Commitment	loose plan, some review	Little more than average
3	70% of time success	3 points of failure	70% Commitment	Panned and Reviewed once	More than average
2	80% of time success	2 points of failure	80% Commitment	Good plan and review	Lots of time
1	90% of time success	1 points of failure	90% Commitment	Solid Plan and Review	3 times average
0	Always Happens	NA	100% Commitment	Rigorous Plan and Review	A ton of time!
Probability of Failure	15	4	8	5	5
35%					

The matrix above will help you look at the variables that impact expectation reality. You can create this tool yourself in a spreadsheet and use it to help you actually mathematically calculate the probability of expectation viability. This one is for the nerds like me that really like to test theories!

The message is simple! Do a check on yourself with regards to expectations. Are you building a house of cards or using steel and concrete? Look back at your own track record of failed and realized expectations, it will tell you a lot! Ask yourself questions about why you expect what you do and what you're willing to put into those expectations in order to make them happen. If you're counting on someone else, you most definitely better check yourself! How reliable is that person? How well do they understand your expectations? How committed are they to delivering their piece of the puzzle?

Asking these questions is work; however, it also can be and usually is a very enlightening event! Hopefully now you, if nothing else, have some thoughts on how to gain greater happiness through building more realistic expectations!

Communicating

Our failure to communicate often becomes one of our largest sources of unhappiness. The questions and feelings we keep inside churn and churn and sometimes surface as storms in our lives.

One of the precepts I've been following for the last few years is to never hold my feelings inside. I find a way to communicate how I feel and what I need to say. We must remember, however to not hastily blurt out our feelings in such a way that they hurt someone else or dig us into a hole.

As I've said before, our words can be remembered and felt by others for a lifetime. While we may be forgiven, some of the things we say will never be really forgotten. I've been reminded of things I said twenty years ago as if I said them yesterday. Despite being twenty years old and a completely different individual at the time, to the person I hurt with my words, it was yesterday and I was still the same guy.

These repercussions may make you scared to communicate, but instead, they should encourage you to communicate carefully and accurately. You see, unresolved issues just aren't good. If you fail to make truth understood, you'll be understood as you are perceived. Think about it for a minute. Twenty years went by and that person still felt pain! It's amazing, isn't it? Anything that causes you twenty years of pain is something you should probably be talking through with someone until you feel enough closure to move on.

A lot of the time, it's hard to have those conversations with people. It takes courage, discipline, self-honesty and a desire to move forward in life. If you don't voice your feelings and expect someone to change or behave differently then you are setting yourself and them up for failure.

Some of what I've written may seem like circular logic. If you have feelings because you are expecting something from someone that they are not capable of delivering, should you communicate those feelings? If you said "no" then you gave the WRONG ANSWER! You need to communicate those feelings as well. You need to tell that person you know it's wrong to expect them to change, but this is how you feel. When you are holding things inside a mood surrounds you and it impacts how other people see you.

Imagine if the way you blew your nose totally freaked somebody out, to the point where they wanted to run away from you. But you don't know they feel this way; they've never mentioned it. All you see is a person who, for no apparent reason, gets mad at you and scampers away. In this example, both people would benefit from better communication. The person who is freaked out could simply say;

"I get really weirded out when you sneeze. I can't help it, so if you see me freak out and scurry off, that's why. I know you can't help the way you sneeze and I don't expect you to change it. I just wanted you to know that I can't help my reaction. I'm working on dealing with it better, but so far I haven't had any luck. It's not really that big of a deal, but I just wanted you to know why I get so weird sometimes."

While it's not exactly what you want to hear, you'll probably feel better knowing why they run off. You might even make an effort to go somewhere else when you feel a sneeze coming on. The person who has the issue will also feel better because they have told you their problem and now have the freedom to deal with the issue without being misunderstood.

Real, honest and thoughtful communication can work for you and others in your life. I suggest you take things a little at a time, making adjustments when you see how those you share with are reacting. Be sure to take accountability for your own feelings as well. Don't assume that the other person needs to change; you always have a role in the overall solution.

How you communicate is also critical. If you talk at people rather than to people you may find yourself being frequently misunderstood. A common thing I see and used to be guilty of is the "it's not my fault you didn't listen" mentality. I hate to chain another ball to your ankle; however, if you want to be understood, it's up to you to communicate effectively.

Consider communication within a marriage. If you don't ensure that your spouse understands what you're saying and acknowledges your point by summarizing it back to you, then you'll probably be disappointed when they don't follow through or act on your words. In addition, we must accept the fact that not everyone will always agree with us and bend to our desires, no matter how effectively we're communicating.

Nevertheless, if you really want to be heard and get your message across, then you must effectively communicate your point. You may need to communicate differently with each person in your life. Do you ever feel that a friend or child is more willing to listen to a stranger's advice than to yours? This is actually true sometimes. Sometimes, the people closest to us are just too close to effectively communicate in a traditional manner.

If you sense you aren't the one who can best communicate a message to someone and you need them to get and understand that message, seriously consider asking someone else to communicate the message on your behalf.

Imagine for a minute that someone in your office has bad breath and every time people talk to them, they feel assaulted. Some people have even mentioned it to them, but they haven't changed. You may try a different approach, like sending an anonymous card and gift. Perhaps the card can be tied to a beautifully wrapped box that, when opened, says: "We all think you're awesome." The person will be elated when they receive it. Perhaps inside the box is another box, and another. And in the last box you have some breath mints and a note wrapped around them that says: "We really do think you're awesome, but your breath is offensive, and we'd really appreciate it if you took corrective action."

Communicating

This is only one example of how you can use a different medium to communicate to someone. It's also a means of adding weight to the message and bringing another level of importance to it. If you want to be understood then it's up to you to ensure you find a way to land your message.

Sharing and communicating can also be very cleansing and healing for you and the others in your life. We previously discussed how things build up and get amplified when there isn't a way to release. Clearing out the attic will really help keep you balanced. It's also a way to achieve higher awareness about yourself, others and life in general.

Remember, if your not being understood, your not being heard!

It's all part of developing A Mind For Life!

Looking ahead, you see more and more detail in the mountains ahead, your ¾'s of the way there. Your journey will end before you expected!

The Smile You Bring Others

This one is really easy! In life we get so caught up in pleasing ourselves that we forget the pure and simple joy that can be experienced by pleasing others.

I learned some time ago that it's more fun to give than receive. Sure there is a balance to this, and even I like to receive something every so often. To me, receiving is more about the thought than the actual gift. I try to apply that same inspiration to the gifts I give others.

People often say it's hard to buy gifts. I agree with this sentiment in regards to buying gifts for people you don't spend much time talking with. If you're buying a gift for your spouse, children, parents or close friends, however, the secret is to simply listen and tune into the things they like and tell you they'd like to have. Often they will like the fact that you listened and sincerely cared enough to get them something that shows you pay attention to them more than they will actually care about the gift itself.

Let me elaborate! Say you're talking with a friend about candy and someone says how much they love Payday candy bars and how they haven't had one in ages. Surprising them with a Payday the next time you see them will surely generate a smile and maybe even a hug! The hardest part of giving the gift will simply be remembering where you last saw one and stopping there to pick it up! Often the gift of our time and attention is the greatest gift of all. Taking the time to find even the smallest of gifts will be recognized and appreciated!

Gifts are often considered great when they're about the person you're buying them for and no one else. The power drill you're thinking about buying your wife, that's not what I am talking about here! Smile! Think about an item which would be a total luxury for the recipient. Perhaps a fine perfume for the lady and a nice bottle of scotch for the gentleman. Something they would never buy for themselves but secretly lust after. That's the kind of gift that will land home and often small luxury items aren't as expensive you'd imagine. History shows that even during hard times, people still buy those items. Small little pleasures!

Giving is a tricky business. All too often we give what we want to give; the gift becomes more about us than the person we're giving it to. When you give, try not to think about what you want. Instead, try thinking about what the person receiving the gift wants.

The Smile You Bring Others

Believe it or not, you can be wrong in not allowing others to give to you as they please rather than as you please. Take Father's Day, for instance. As a dad you might think that you should get gifts that you like and that the day should be all about you. But making your children feel good about what they gave you, regardless of whether you like it is more important than getting something you wanted. It may even be what Father's Day is really about. Remember, any acknowledgement from your children that you are their father and they love you is more valuable than any gift you could ever receive. The same goes for Mother's Day!

Life can be tough if you expect that being a great gift-giver means you should automatically receive great gifts. You can easily become very unhappy and disappointed. Perhaps in these times you can focus on the people who care about you and remember that it's really about the thought and not the gift.

Perspective is like the devil in the details. Some moms are happy to just receive a call from their child on Mother's Day, while others see it as being lazy or too cheap to buy a gift. It's all about perspective!

It's about the energy we create towards others. I remember someone once telling me that I never smiled and always looked grumpy. When they confronted me they actually realized I was nice and not grumpy at all - I only looked that way. They saw me smile one time and said I had a really nice smile. For quite some time after that day I tried smiling and acknowledging others around me more often. The sheer act of me smiling caused others to smile. A smile from you creates smiles in others.

A Mind for Life

Smiles are an energy source. I realize that this may sound too new wave. However, I really have proven this theory in practice. Your smile goes a long way towards making others smile and when everyone is smiling it means people are feeling good and are generally happier. Someone once told me it takes more muscles and energy to frown than it does to smile. I'm not sure if this is technically true, however, in a practical sense, it rings true for me. Try smiling more often and see what it brings and means to others. Say good morning! Tell your spouse and children you love them!

I believe that happiness can really be about the smile you bring others! Give it a try, it's really addictive and, remember, it's not only about you, it's as much about them!

Rose Candles

Mark Abraham
The Apartment 2008

Two hearts burn brighter than candles; the love and its sweetness glow like a rose in the flickering candlelight! I am so very grateful for the special lady in my life who is my partner in the great ride of life! Memories of espresso and great conversation are forever etched in my mind and heart!

We Are Who We Are

One of the most difficult aspects of A Mind For Life is dealing with the notion of the desire for self change that your newly gained awareness may bring. After all, we are who we are; a lion is a lion and it's a lion's nature to hunt, kill and feed. How can we be anything different if, despite our efforts to change, we're compelled to follow our true nature?

If we have an inherent need for attention, power and material objects, how will change effect those characteristics? Will those desires go away? The honest answer is no, they will probably never completely go away. They can, however, fade over time if we really work to change.

One of the most difficult stereotypes to understand is the addict. Regardless of their addiction, be it booze, drugs, alcohol or gambling, an addict never stops craving the perceived sweet fruits of their addiction. An addict will attempt to fulfill their cravings to their own demise. Even though society doesn't label it as such, many other issues parallel addiction. For example, people can clearly be addicted to attention, power or love.

Much of what I've talked about and will later discuss is focused on either limiting our expectations or making more realistic expectations. Let's key in on the latter and apply it to a situation where someone in a relationship needs to receive lots of attention.

If we are the way we are and we are a person that seeks and craves a lot of attention then we should make sure we choose a life partner with a doting nature. It's funny that when two people meet they often think they aren't compatible with each when, in reality, they are!

Nature has a cruel way of playing with us when it comes to this. Take for example a guy and gal meeting each other for coffee. Let's say the gal is the kind of gal that loves affection. On a scale of 1-10 with 10 representing a person that needs a tremendous amount of attention and 1 being a person that needs no attention at all, she's a 7. On a similar scale, tracking how much attention we like to pay to our partners, the guy is also 7. He'll look to tend to many of his gal's needs!

But when they meet, the gal thinks the guy is overbearing. Well Houston, therein lies the problem! The gal might see him as annoying, but he's probably at his peak of 10 trying to show how caring he is and the gal is at a 5 on her scale, trying not to seem high maintenance. The gal doesn't give the guy her number and moves forward, still looking for a guy that will be a 6 or 7 when she meets him. She may then marry that guy who later returns to his normal self, which was a 4. She returns to her true nature of wanting a 7 and becomes somewhat unhappy with the amount of attention she receives.

This illustrates the importance of being yourself while you're courting. More importantly, it shows us how important it is to act like ourselves in order to gain a true understanding of and awareness about our nature. If you don't understand who you really are and make use of that awareness, you can create a lot of problems for yourself. It's also a key factor in deciding whether you should remain in a relationship. If your relationship was built on a lie where you both pretended to be people you weren't and you have no desire to be those two people again, then your relationship will become a constant source of unhappiness.

Let's get back to our example. So, is our gal too needy? She's a 7 on a scale of 10 and while it's a bit high, she might be able to manage with a guy who's a 5 or 6. If she were a 10, however, she might want to look at how she can survive with less attention.

Measuring yourself and understanding whether your true nature on any particular issue is a source of pain to you partially answers some of the great questions we've previously posed. Another part of that equation is to learn to understand the relevance of your nature towards your overall happiness. Perhaps there is something you crave a lot but receive little of in your life. Despite this absence, however, if all the other pillars of importance in your life are fulfilled, your overall house of happiness will seem and feel stable.

We have to see ourselves as honestly as we possibly can. Again, true self-awareness is key to achieving A Mind For Life.

A Mind for Life

Sometimes, just like recovering addicts, we have to negotiate with ourselves in order to resist our impulses and suppress our true natures for our overall health. Most people are already aware that addictions can be hazardous to our continued existence. The key is to be realistic and fair with regards to understanding who you really are and what makes you tick. Once you do that, you can decide what changes you want to make and are willing to work for.

Remember, transcending to greater happiness we requires awareness of not only ourselves but also others.

Feeling The Love

Love and devotion are like the pendulum on the clock of time, swaying back and forth but always moving time forward. We make friends; we have best friends; we take lovers; we sometimes transcend beyond love to a higher form of friendship full of love and devotion. Love is possessive by nature and while it can be blissful it can also breed selfishness and jealousy.

I believe higher forms of love are unselfish. In those relationships, we place those we love before ourselves, even at personal cost. Love is essential to the human spirit as it brings stability to our lives. We seek to hold on to love for as long as we can since there is no other feeling quite like it. To reject love is to kill one's spirit. We must also have and respect love of ourselves as it is critical to our existence. We must love and be at peace with ourselves before we can love others.

A Mind for Life

I feel funny about including a chapter on love in this book, but it wouldn't be complete without it. Love and its significance are essential to understanding A Mind For Life. As humans, we aren't complete without love. Love is also not what completes us as our totality embodies all our emotions. So much of how we behave and are guided is based on love. Whether it be love of another, love of ourselves or some combination of the two, love is there and it's extremely powerful.

As with all of my passages in life meanings there is a reason why this one came to exist. So much of what challenges us in life seems circular when we stop and think about it. I've personally been in a situation where I questioned whether real love meant letting go or holding on.

To be honest, we could enter and exit this topic and get absolutely nowhere towards answering that question. If you are willing to let go of someone, do you really love them? If you won't let them go even though you know they want you to, do you really love them? Can you put their needs ahead of your own?

Publicly, people have obvious answers to these questions and might even be outraged if someone dared to ask. Deep inside, however, people struggle with these types of questions because our sense of self is often stronger than our love of anyone else.

When I got off the bus in boot camp, I remember being told that our priorities should be God, then family, then country. If we love God then we should follow the will of God before all else. If we love another person the most we possibly can, shouldn't we put them ahead of ourselves? And yet, if we really love someone, how can we possibly let go?

Feeling The Love

Love is not so black and white; I don't believe the answer is satisfied with a simple yes or no. In life, we have to be able to consider and navigate through the gray areas. I believe we can let go even when our heart and spirit really don't want to. We can also hang on and not let those we love go. In moments like these, people do the best they can. When we are faced with impossible choices we must make a choice and live with the consequences.

Can a person truly love two people, or is there only room for one? When it comes to children we can love more than one and love them equally. When it comes to romance, I personally believe there is only one true love. My gut tells me that if I thought that I loved two different women, I probably didn't truly love either of them. And so it is with life in general and with regards to making absolute decisions. Another way to look at this is from the other side. If the person you were in love with loved two people, how would you feel?

Jealousy is a fascinating emotion. Do you want your partner to be jealous if another person is chasing after your affections, or do you believe they shouldn't be jealous if they love and believe in you? People could endlessly debate this question. There isn't a right answer; it's simply more gray matter to navigate.

I also want to talk about a few relationship dynamics in this chapter. In my opinion, many people in marriages and serious relationships take each other for granted. I believe this can eventually lead to serious relationship problems, because as people we are inherently selfish, we like to receive more than we think about giving.

When we meet someone and fall in love, we look and act a certain way. In return, we want our partner to love us for who we are. Since we are human, we naturally adapt and change as our lives play out. Some things in us change for the better and others for the worse. Keep in mind that a good change for you might be seen as a bad change for someone else. When it comes down to it, we prefer little change in others.

I have gained some serious weight a few times in my life and when I do that I make myself less desirable. At the very least I become different. If our attitudes and demeanors change, we also become different. Perhaps we let our hair down so to speak, or maybe our tempers and bad habits become more evident. We are programmed to believe that love should survive and transcend all these things. In reality, however, these changes often alienate us from each other.

If you've been in a relationship, I'm sure that after a while you found things out about your partner that you didn't like or bothered you. We seldom flip the other way around and think about how our significant other sees us and our faults too. Again, when it comes to being loved, we want that love to be unconditional. We have a double standard.

These are not exactly new things I'm talking about; however, they're particularly critical in relationships. It's why it's so important to be who you are early on in a relationship in order to let the other person know how you'll be as the relationship progresses. To that end, one way we can give to the ones we love is to be as constant or dynamic as they need. We can keep ourselves fit and healthy. Healthy not only in body, but also in mind, so that we remain the kind, sweet person our significant other fell in love with.

Feeling The Love

When we court another person and they court us, we tend to be at our best. If we viewed this graphically and imposed a comfort zone into the graph we would see that in a successful courtship we sit on the high side of the acceptance and comfort zone of the other person.

As time passes, we begin to gravitate towards our normal, real self. Where that positions us in the acceptance and comfort zone for our loved one often goes unconsidered. If we dip below the sweet spot then our relationship will begin to unravel. All too often we carry the notion that we'll be unconditionally loved. That's simply not a very realistic concept. We have a role in maintaining a successful relationship and catering to the needs and desires of our partner.

Letting too many things slide takes a toll on our partners. That's why I believe it's really nice to let our significant other know that we won't take them for granted. It shows our love and dedication. This why being real and ourselves early on makes it far easier to have a successful, long-lasting relationship. If you falsely capture another person's heart, the truth will eventually become known and your relationship will suffer greatly.

This may be hard to digest, and you shouldn't take my words to extremes. I'm not suggesting you never burp in front of your spouse or that you never gain weight. I'm suggesting, however, that making relationships work takes effort on both people's parts. When it comes to the ones we love most, we should really keep an eye out for how much we ask and take the other for granted.

Of course, communication is the key!! Letting your significant other know how you feel and any problems you have in a kind and loving way is important. If you don't let your partner know how you're feeling and the expectations you have around those feelings, you're setting the two of you up for failure. They may never know that you want something to change and, therefore, never have the opportunity to acknowledge its importance to you and change. It can be complicated.

When we love others we need to show them and make sure they always believe we care and love them. I believe love is a circle of giving and caring. The more we care about someone and the more we give to them, the more they care about us and want to give back. This can become a self-perpetuating circle that keeps building energy if we stay true to the path.

It's amazing how the little things can mean so much to a person. Bringing your husband or wife a cup of coffee in the morning or doing their laundry or another chore for them shows real love. A glass of cold water when someone is working hard outside is a sure sign of care! On the flip side, it's important to acknowledge our partner's little acts of kindness, even if it's something you didn't ask for or want. Too often we take those things for granted. People give in different and personal ways. We need awareness to understand how people give to us. We also need awareness to understand what our significant other likes to receive.

Listening can be invaluable in understanding this equation. Letting your significant other know what means something to you and what doesn't will help you avoid a crash in expectations. At the same time, it's important to be selfless and open enough to understand that sometimes we need to accept a person's gift without worrying about whether we like it. It's a funny loop, but sometimes we give by allowing others to give!

Feeling The Love

We also need to be careful to not build a person up to someone they aren't in our mind. The human mind is such that a person can literally create and fall in love with a physical person who really doesn't even exist. In this case, you're in love with the idea of the person you created and probably haven't even taken time to understand who they really are. Perhaps it was their sweet looks or something like that which drew you to them in the first place. Please keep in mind that this person might actually be a kind, nice person in reality even if they aren't the kind of person you'd love if you really knew them. When the fantasy starts to unravel, we are more apt to blame the person who isn't who we expected them to be.

This is yet another reason why self-awareness is so critical to happiness. It's often the difference between living an illusion and realistically existing with balance.

Many ask, won't you know true love when you find it? My answer is, maybe! What may seem like love today may seem like a misplaced notion in the future. With the divorce rate as high as it is in the United States, it's hard to conclude otherwise. My conclusion is that in most cases people who get divorced didn't know each other very well to begin with, had unrealistic expectations of each other or simply grew apart over time.

In order to truly love another, you must be happy with and, yes, love yourself. While that may seem conceited, I really don't mean it that way.

If we can't find happiness within ourselves, it will be hard to find it with someone else. In addition to loving yourself, you also need to be content with your life. If you love yourself and your partner, but hate your life then you'll still likely be unhappy. I believe that developing A Mind For Life and the self-awareness and inner peace that can result from it positions us better to be able to experience true love with others.

It's about being able to look in the mirror, smile and feel good about who you are and how you're managing life. Life will never be easy; that's why keeping life simple leads to greater happiness. There is less to unravel and less to get upset about. It's easier to enjoy your relationship when life isn't stealing your attention away from happiness.

When we can feel all others and all things, we experience a sense of oneness. Maybe it's the stare of a woman sitting at a traffic light with the rain coming down and glimpsing her face in the side mirror through rivets of rain. She's lost in her thoughts. She looks pensive, distant, and almost oblivious to the status of the traffic light. She's thinking and feeling life and so am I as I watch from my own car. And yet, somehow, when the light changes we're all aware enough to remove our feet from the breaks, step on the gas pedals and propel forward. We hear the tires treading through the damp concrete below, and we continue on to our destination. This is a small example of experiencing oneness with our life, world, circumstances and others.

Some of these moments lost in the abyss are more pleasant than others. There might have been a guy to your side, smiling, sipping coffee and mouthing the words to a song, having no care or regard for the that fact that it's raining. He, like the woman in the car, is tied into the pulse of life; he, too, moves forward when the light changes.

Feeling The Love

To love is to know and feel good about your place in the world. It's to know that everyday won't be the same; some will be good, some will be bad. It might be about the gratitude of having a wife and family at home. Maybe it's having a dog to greet you at the door, because that's where you are at in life. Maybe it's just a TV and having a place to call home. Maybe it's a person rolling down their window to give a homeless man some food; for that man, it's just the gratitude of having a meal.

One thing we find hard to understand and respect in relationships is that everyone needs their space. The definition of space can be quite broad. Whether it be time alone or their own private thoughts, people need their space.

It occurs to me that we find this need hard to honor. We don't want those closest to us to have secrets, but everyone does. It's important to honor other people's need for space. We often have the proverbial double standard when it comes to our own need and desire for space.

When we're close to someone we often want to know everything about them. But people aren't perfect and knowing all about someone's past or mistakes leads to disappointment.

A person's need for space can also feel like rejection. It's very hard to balance this in relationships. Nonetheless, I believe it must be done. If a person gives up their space, they give up a huge piece of themselves. If you drive them to do so then you are taking away their shelter. If you study psychology you'll find that shelter is one of our higher basic needs. While many people equate this to physical shelter like a house or roof over someone's head, it can also be mental shelter –a place where we can retreat to when things get difficult. The message here is short and simple. Allow others and yourself some space!

Life is love! For most people it's, unknowingly, the greatest love affair of all. It's ourselves and our place in that life that keeps us living. Self-love allows us to carry on no matter how good or bad life is at the moment. Perhaps we even compare our love of ourselves to our love of others in order to ascertain just how much love we have and who it's for. What I do know is the more situated and accepting we are of ourselves and life in general, the greater our capacity to love others.

You may need to embrace and live a material life in order to please people you love. You could mostly decouple yourself from material needs such as a large house or an expensive car, be tempted to sell all of it off for something simpler and easier to maintain and end up causing considerable grief for those you love.

Studies are showing that people are finding great comfort in reducing their material dependence and moving their focus towards living life and making memories. These studies show that people increasingly prefer travel as opposed to big homes and fancy cars. Personally, I believe this is great, but travel and small luxuries can become a pacifier for larger needs. Still, simplifying is the right answer; the more we simplify the easier it all gets. To be truly free we need to rid ourselves of these needs completely, not simply suppress them. This takes serious effort and reprogramming to accomplish.

Remember to be careful in both your enthusiasm and expectations as you move forward. If you are truly building A Mind For

Feeling The Love

Life then you are embracing the fact that others may not and you are also finding a way to easily coexist with them anyway.

Love is not logical. It can't be rationalized, justified, or even quantified. Maybe the answer is that Love Just IS.

Looking up, you're surprised to see that your destination is so close you feel you could run to the finish line!

Happiness Comes and Goes

No matter what great logic we apply and implement, happiness will always be fleeting.

A Mind For Life attempts to build a mindset that transcends beyond the highs and lows we all experience.

The one gift I believe God seems to give most of us is the spirit to move on. We've talked about the lies we tell ourselves, the twisting of reality and the many secret ways our mind works. Think about the following examples. Consider a starving person; they appear skinny as a rail and have no idea where their next meal will come from or when it's coming. Then compare them to a person who makes a dramatic event out of their order being wrong at a restaurant.

Perspective is so significant. Our ability to make and break ourselves and the awareness of it all is seemingly invisible. What it all boils down to, in my mind, is awareness. The ability to see when it's okay to let ourselves enter survival mode when the chips are down and still be able to smile and enjoy life when it's good!

I'll share with you a few secrets that will probably ring strong for some of you and be too difficult for others to accept. I encourage you to reduce your need for material happiness. It's expensive; not only in monetary terms but also on the long-term toll it takes on your happiness.

Americans are a highly debt driven society. We borrow until it causes us to lose sleep. Think about how much easier you'd sleep if you were debt free. A tip I offer is to try and reduce your debt to only your house and car. If you can do more, balance it against other investments. For example, you may want to decide if putting extra money in your house has greater long-term good than other investments. The same goes for your car.

Often we pay a huge price for things we see as status symbols or believe will make us happy. Take a luxury car, for example. How long does the high of owning a fancy car last? Know yourself when it comes to these things and take time to think about the long-term value of the materials you buy. $50,000 or more on a car is a lot of jack. Most people only keep cars for four or five years. After five years, in many cases, the car is worth very little of your original investment. I'm not trying to give you a financial seminar in one chapter, so I'll shorten this up.

If you can get your house right side up, meaning you can sell it and make enough to clear capital gains, move and get started

Happiness Comes and Goes

somewhere else, you'll sleep easier and be more prepared for downturns in your life. If your monthly payments are something you can afford to make even if you lose your job and have to take a salary cut, then getting laid off won't be so scary. Maybe you'll have more fun year to year taking a $5000 vacation and owning a reasonable car than you would driving the luxury car everyday. You may create more fond memories, as well.

What about all that material junk we collect? How does the prospect of cleaning your cellar or garage feel? Have you ever really tried to clear out the junk you've collected? It's harder than you think! That garage sale you're thinking of having, it won't get rid of everything, nor will it make you as much money as you thought it would. If you think about getting rid of old junk before buying new junk, you'll vastly simplify your life.

Look forward to enjoying the simple things. Watch a sunset, go to a ball game, or take the family on a picnic. Savor the moments a lot more and the materialism a lot less. Think about other things you can do or memories you can make verses the amount of time you can sink into the television. How fondly will you reflect back on that episode of Survivor in five years? Probably not as much as the holiday you had in Europe.

If it helps, think of the evil, genius puppet master that is pulling your strings causing you to want and desire material things so much. Think about the puppet master laughing at you when it sees how fast your enjoyment fades and how long and hard you work to pay for it. You are that puppet master; don't forget how much pain you create for yourself by not being able to say no!

A Mind for Life

I'm not prescribing how to live; I'm just suggesting that you take time to think about what's really important to you. Personally, I pass more frequently on the superficial things in life. Try saying yes to the more spiritually generating aspects of life. Don't take it too far, however. You don't have to become a Tibetan monk in order to find true happiness. As I've said before, the best path usually lies between the extremes.

When you're feeling down, take some time and reflect on why you feel that way. Ask yourself the hard questions. Look in the mirror and ask how you allowed yourself to get there. Think about what would truly make things better and then start taking small steps towards that goal.

Finally, if you need to forgive yourself for your past life - do it. Tell those you wronged you're sorry. Swallow the shallow pride you are holding on to and free yourself from the prison you've built around you. Say sorry to the people who wronged you and who you may have regrets for how you responded or how it impacted others. Take accountability for the decisions you've made and the actions you have taken.

Try making plans that make you feel like you can make up for whatever you feel guilty about. Address the regrets you have; then march forth! You'll feel better! Yes, it'll be hard! Try taking small steps and don't look back for awhile.

Lower Falls
Mark Abraham
Yellowstone National Park 2005

Standing in the distance, taking a picture. A lady asked me what I was doing; I replied I was taking a picture for my book. She asked what kind of book; I replied an inspirational book. Perhaps this book is not that book and then again, maybe it is!

My Life Now

You're justified in wondering what qualifies me to write this book. I'm sure you're curious about my life and what's so great about it? Many of my readers know me and think that my life looks very normal. I work, I have the same pains many others do, I am not financially independent; the list goes on and on.

I am not perfect and I definitely have made and still make mistakes. The path I'm currently on will seem immensely insane to many of you. I am not even trying to be perfect because I don't really believe perfection is necessary. Simply speaking, I seek to be rich in spirit, not in wealth!

This is a conscious choice - not a failure. I've received many appealing offers and turns in the road that I chose not to take because my health and spirit were more important to me. I've also made some mistakes along the way. I feel grateful to have learned all that I have at such a young age. I've often been humbled by life and the consequences of my own ignorance.

My grandfather and father were amazing men, each in their own and often contrasting ways. I learned to take parts from both of them. I made a choice to emulate what I liked about each of them and avoid what I didn't like.

Everyday I'm getting better at processing what's really relevant to my life versus what's just a part of the superficial materialized world we currently live in.

The modern reality we live today and the reality each person has lived in the past might be likened to a house. It's a building we physically enter and live in each day. Our mind, however, isn't contained in the house, nor can reality itself consume and contain our mind. Our physical and mental environments and landscapes are very different if we allow them to be. Would you rather your mind live within your physical environment or beyond the limits of your surroundings?

I cherish time with the ones I love, great sunsets, longs walks, paths with nature on all sides and taking time to think about life and savor the quiet simplicity that is abundantly found in reflections. I truly enjoy oneness!

From the outside, many people might look at my life and say it's no different from anyone else's. I probably wouldn't take any time or effort to debate their opinions. My house and physical life look like most others. Where we really live and exist, however, is in our own minds. It's truly all about how I feel inside and the way I choose to view and live life. My goal with regards to the material aspects of life is to reduce my footprint. I opt out of achieving the material dream far more than I opt into it!

I hope this book helps you find your own inner peace and happiness. Don't look for perfection, however, because the way we've been taught to understand and view perfection is imperfect in my opinion. Smile!

Just Relax

It came to me, as I walked by a person who looked all tense sitting in their office reading e-mail, I wanted to just go and tell them to loosen up and relax a bit.

As I said earlier, I too used to go to work feeling tense and ready for battle. Then things happened, my life changed and I realized that being tense all the time wasn't worth it. It was a complete waste of my time and energy. If ever there's an example of self-manufactured programming, this is it!

Think about all the times we get tense! It might be traffic jams, for example. Instead of becoming stressed, I finally started laughing at traffic jams and using them as opportunities to relax and think. Whenever I'm in a traffic jam I instantly have awareness and don't even let myself go to that bad place the sight of stalled traffic can take us to! Instead, I smile, adjust my iPod to some good music, make sure I am comfortable in my seat and just settle in for a while. It makes a huge difference in my attitude when I finally walk in my front door and greet my family.

Failing to address tension leaves us drained. If, during a traffic jam, we cursed, lamented, honked, jockeyed in and out of traffic and tried to force our way out of the gridlock, we would feel drained and tense when we arrive home. We might still be raving about the traffic when we walk in the door and, instead of a warm smile, our family would be greeted by an angry person.

Our muscles can get sore; our neck can ache and cause headaches. Even our faces can get tense and then droopy! The list goes on! Tension is mostly self-manufactured! We get tense due to other's expectations of us and we really need to work and temper this reactions - it's simply not worth the toll it takes. Often we didn't even create those expectations; others created them for and often without us and then imposed them upon us.

As always, begin to gain awareness by asking yourself questions!

Why am I so tense?
Is it worth it?
Is someone causing me to feel this way or is it myself?
Is this healthy?
What can I do to be more relaxed?
Do I need to simplify my life in order to reduce my stress level?
Do I need to communicate with others in order to help them help me reduce my stress level?

The questions above are a jumping off point; there are many others you can ask as well. Once you consistently adopt this method of dealing with your negative emotions you'll get to a point where you ask yourself less questions and learn to change gears instantly. After all, in our traffic example, once you go through the process a few times, what's the point of continuing to ask yourself the same questions? The answers won't change and you'll soon realize that those kinds of negative emotions are just a waste of your time and energy!

One of the key benefits to A Mind For Life is that you eventually do end up feeling more relaxed and less bothered. You start to savor the good moments and push away the futile bad emotions that we are programmed to keep repeating over and over!

Let go of all that tension and find your mind for life! Let go and relax!

What Now?

I've had a lot of fun writing A Mind For Life. Hopefully, you've enjoyed the journey as well. When people ask me about my photography and ask who I take pictures for, I tell them I take the pictures for myself and feel fortunate when others also enjoy them. I feel the same way about this book. I love to write down my thoughts and I've learned a lot by sorting through and exploring them in order to form this book. This has been a journey for me, too! I hope turning the last page of A Mind For Life will mean something. To be honest, the more I write and capture, the more new thoughts leap into my mind. At some point, however, I needed to stop!

At the end of the day, I had a few goals for this book. I wanted to share with you the notion of programming and the fact that it has a tremendous impact on our lives. I hoped to share with you ways to see the programming and to encourage you to choose your own path.

Not all programming is bad; I've shared this with you already. It's my hope that you now have a place to start to recognize it, explore it and selectively filter out what you want.

I wanted to liberate you and not brainwash you. In a way, it's comical to write a book on how to undo brainwashing and describe methods which, in essence, could be considered a new form of brainwashing.

My goal was to explore thoughts with you that I've already partially explored myself. Hopefully, my words will stimulate your own thinking about how you see life and about your overall level of awareness. Perhaps you will subscribe to some of my ideas and reject others.

I ask you to consider that many of the great questions about our existence go unasked and therefore unconsidered. Awareness and enlightenment come from asking lots of questions and exploring for answers. This is how we've come to make so many revelations about our universe!

I used to display my work at cafes and I would sometimes sit there anonymously and watch people interact with my art, soaking in their comments and reflections. It was a true learning experience and it caused me to develop a true appreciation of many diverse people and the different ways they see and think about things.

To that end, these words are here for you to either accept or reject as you choose. If they make you think at all then I'll feel very successful. Visit my website if you have time and drop me an e-mail on your thoughts if you like!

What Now?

Next I am going to talk about finding your path. Many of you will find this section abstract and confusing. Maybe someday I'll write another book or blog to explore the notion further. Take some time, let go! I mean really, really let go and let your mind flow. It's okay to disengage for a while and sort yourself out.

Hopefully, if you've taken your time with this book, you'll have done just that and be ready and eager to do more. Sort it all out and find your path!

You have now arrived at your destination and if you look back the distance looks as great as it did when you started. Fortunately, you don't have to return to the other side, unless you let the current carry you there like a feather in the wind. From time to time, your inner puppet master will try to push you back to where you started. Whether it succeeds is up to you.

Closing

I hope you'll gain some wisdom from my words. If you seriously want to make changes then begin taking notes by writing down the things you want to change and revisit that list regularly.

A more frequent awareness of what you want to change will begin with you pausing whenever unwanted behavior or thought processes initiate. The more you learn, the easier it gets to resist your built-in programming. You'll begin to write your own programs and, in time, those programs might begin to map out your new life path. These new programs will encompass a new way of thinking and will lead you toward a new life and greater happiness. As you go on, things will get easier.

I hope you liked the openness with which I have written this book. I believe I've left you to choose and shape your own life. I hope that some of the personal introspect I've offered have provided you with living, breathing examples of how we can choose to think differently and the difference that can make in our lives.

This isn't really the last chapter, thus the chapter title Closing is a bit misplaced. I want to leave you with the following words resonating in your mind. In my mind, they are the next part of A Mind For Life. What has proceeded is worthy of a complete book in itself and so what follows might be considered as fodder for the future.

Thanks for taking this walk with me. I hope it's been an enjoyable experience and that maybe our paths will cross again. Thanks again, and may you find A Mind For Life!

Arch Stairs
Mark Abraham
Arches National Park 2007

We climb upwards, full of hope and promise. The path feels steady and true beneath our feet and in our heart! The view beyond the arch opens upon new horizons.

The Path

This book has been fairly straight forward and logical up until now. Watch very carefully, however, because I'm throwing you a curve ball! The Path, as I call it, is one of the more difficult concepts I refer to in my writings. It's complicated to describe which, in turn, makes it even more difficult to grasp and understand.

You may be able to apply the concept of The Path to your own life, no matter what faith you follow. I can't really say that with any certainty and I by no means wish to offend anyone. In that spirit, I am not sure what mischief I'll get myself in writing this chapter. At the risk of alienating some readers, I'll share my abstract thoughts on the Path. The core nature of this belief revolves around simplicity and since most faiths have deep historic roots, hopefully I won't offend anyone.

A Mind for Life

Imagine for a moment that you're in a white room with nothing but you and your thoughts about life. There are no distractions or material possessions to get in your way. There is just you and the present time. No phones, televisions, people, absolutely nothing - just you and your thoughts. If you prefer, it might be helpful to think of this place as a cloud. The idea is to feel that this place has no bearing on you and generates no thought or reaction from the location itself. There is no fear or joy, not even wonderment as to where you are. Specifically, the place is transparent. You exist without an environment.

A person has a disposition all times, despite everything and everyone around them. To be specific, in a place that is transparent and that contains no one to think about or interact with, you still have a mood. It's almost comical to think about how different people might react and feel in a place and state of nothing. Some would be happy, some reflective, some sad, some angry, and so on and so forth. In short, despite our environment we have a disposition and that underlying disposition follows us from location to location.

I hope you're still following me here, because this is really abstract in nature. It might take a bit to get to the heart of what I really mean and where I am going.

If a hundred people in such a place and state can feel a hundred ways then, to me, that indicates that we have free choice of our emotions despite our environment and surroundings. You might be saying, "Well, duh!" right now and that reaction is, in itself, part of what limits us and ultimately leaves us controlled by our programming rather than a result of our desires and free wills. Your response is partially influenced by your current disposition. Smile!

The Path

Why does one person get to be happy and another angry? While this may make many uncomfortable, it's by choice; a failure to live freely becomes the genesis of the answer to our question. The sad, angry people with negative dispositions have chosen (consciously or unconsciously) to reside in that state by remaining controlled by their programming. An extension of this thought would be to consider that God gives us all life equally, it is a gift and we are granted the capacity to make choices that impact our lives, our beliefs in God and the ability in large part to choose how we will live.

In part, programming is all the input that has led us to act and be as we are at this point and time. If we have awareness then we have a choice, and we can decide consciously rather than be ruled by our unconscious, which is a reflection originating from the sum of our life. That statement is a half-truth of sorts, as we'll always be impacted by our unconscious; it's not something we can control. It's something we can influence and reshape over time with new programming.

The path, as I call it, is literally a path. You can form an image of it in your mind. Close your eyes, clear your mind, and see your path. Clearing the mind is the secret and it is one of the most difficult of disciplines to learn. Perhaps yoga or meditation can help you with the state of mind it takes to see your path. Coincidentally, I've never explored either of these disciplines, so I would contend you don't absolutely need them in order to get there. The entry to the path is the equivalent of the state we reach right before we fall asleep or begin to daydream. It's the instant before the dream when our brain pauses, ends one activity and begins a new one.

A Mind for Life

For me, the path is real. I once had an experience where I found myself on the path while I was dreaming. When I awoke, that notion of the path was validated through what can only be considered coincidence. The validation came three times in my life, the final one in the moment of my father's passing where his last conscious words to me were that he was just following the path. Incidentally, my father and I never spoke of such things or about much of anything of spiritual substance. I'm not sure you've ever experienced coming to know something and felt how it sits in both your mental and physical being. This, however, is how the path is fixed in me. For me, there is no doubt. There is no physical proof and I don't require any. It is simply my truth.

I'll give you some clues before you try to find your path. Your path is likely quiet, easy, peaceful, simple, uncluttered, beautiful and calm. While this might sound like a meditation technique, I promise you it's not. Your path visually accessed in your mind is individualistic and yet simple. A hyper person might find this extremely hard to believe and, therefore, difficult to visualize and access because they may be too impatient to believe that a quiet, calm place can even exist in their mind.

You can't see very far forward or backward as you stand upon your path. That is the way the path is, and I believe it's by design. Imagine that the distance is blurred and out of focus. It feels and seems like the deeper you try to see ahead or behind you the foggier the distance appears. If you think or question it too hard, your path simply disappears.

At first, the path can be very hard to see because it's not frequently traveled. Instead, there are thousands of trails (diversions if you

The Path

will) crossing over it. Some people weave back and forth over the path but spend little time actually following it.

The one path (your path) is overlaid or superimposed over or beneath all the trails.

If you imagine that the path has a different feeling and positive mood when followed and is quiet, happy and calm you might liken it to moments of strong, simple happiness in your life.

I'll share one such vision. I was tired and weary when I woke one morning. Holding a hot cup of coffee and smelling the aroma as I cupped it in my hands to my face and feeling the warmth and heat of the mug radiate through my fingers and hands literally brought warmth and comfort to my bones. I was thinking about how fortunate I was and how I wanted to embrace life even more.

That simple moment, just a few seconds in time, was a moment on the path. I was just me, warmth, and appreciation for this simple, hot vessel of liquid cupped in my hands. It breathed life and energy into me, and I was able to move on.

In these moments we really don't worry about looking ahead or thinking about the past. We simply exist in the moment from second to second. We are ourselves and empowered by a sense of oneness to be all that we can. In this way, the path ahead and behind is blurry and not really relevant.

It's so hard to stay on the path, even when you close your eyes and see it clearly. The path forgets the past and allows the future to dynamically unfold as it is needed.

In that moment with my coffee; a siren outside, a plane above, or any other of a thousand events could've interrupted my moment and finding it again would've been nearly impossible. Many people weave off the path onto the side trails. In reality, a lot of us end up spending 99% of our time on other trails full of our own demands and complexities.

I do believe that the path, as I call it, is revealed when you are able to disengage from the materially programmed life we live. It can't be seen unless we let go of what we've been taught and begin to just feel and absorb what is the simple, unique truth.

I guess it's important to note here that you don't have to float off on a white cloud in order to be on the path. You could be driving, working, working out or doing any number of other activities that are tied to the material world. The point is that they aren't truly occupying your forward movement when you're on the path. It might be easy to say that when you are not on the path everything else in life that isn't true or real is holding you still and preventing you from moving forward on the path.

I work to support my family; I do a great job at work. I can be at work submerged in all of its demanding details and still be on my path. That shows me that work is part of my journey and it is what provides for my family and me. If my job were forcing me to be a bad person or harm others, I wouldn't be able to be on my path because I know my path is about honesty, compassion and truth.

An easier way to describe the path is simply having one of those moments where you just feel great to be alive and a smile comes across your face. If asked, "Why are you smiling?" you wouldn't know how to answer other than to reply, "I just feel great." When

The Path

the material world grabs us we most often wander off our path. Modern life practically demands we not be able to follow the path for very long, unless we are to neglect our upkeep, nutrition and shelter. Reality mandates that we care about our connection to the physical world, even though we live in our minds.

Through some reflection and effort, you can meld your real world and path together so they are mostly one. I realize that this is difficult to comprehend; it will become more clear if you work and experience it for yourself.

It's important to note that while I paint a picture of the path being the ultimate and only true thing in our lives, the human mind probably isn't capable of ever being on the path one hundred percent of the time. If a person mediated all day they wouldn't be able to provide food, water and shelter to satisfy their physical needs. There is our body which is the physical keeper and essential house to the mind. Our mind and our non-physical heart are the conduits to our spirit. If you care to take things one step further - our spirit is our conduit to our soul which must be developed for eternity. When we work with integrity and honesty, perhaps to provide for our families, we can feel our path close by and know our labor is good.

This is a great time to explain my views on the meaning of life. I, like countless others, have pondered the subject. I think when I started life meanings I hoped that by writing thoughts down I might stumble upon the answer to the grand question.

I think the reason why the meaning of life is so elusive is simply this: it's different from person to person and moment to moment. Seeking the meaning of life is a little like trying to shoot a bug that's flying Mach 5 while you're blind folded using a sling shot with a bee-bee as your bullet!

If we accept that the meaning of life may be unique and dynamic, then we might land with the notion of a path rather than a single static answer. If you embrace and accept the fact that we are all different for a reason, it becomes easier to understand. We are all essential parts to a greater whole that transcends us and our unique existence.

A path leads places and is something that is travelled. It affords movement and progression towards a destination. Some of you probably wonder where the path leads, Unfortunately, my answer may seem stark and harsh. The path begins when we are born and ends when we cease to exist in the minds of all others. I guess this also means that the path and life can be eternal if you believe in God and that you'll always exist in the mind of God. If you don't believe in God, perhaps it will be as long as you last in the minds of others.

What I am suggesting is that your life meaning unfolds on the path and that it's not just about you. It's beyond you. That can either be comforting or discomforting. As with most of this book, it's up to you to decide how you want to see it.

If you are purely scientific by nature then I will propose you look at it from the vantage point of subatomic particle. What if that particle wondered what its purpose was? The answer might be that its purpose is to be a part of something else. If you don't accept this answer because you think as humans we are special then you may need to reconsider your beliefs about God because it's the

The Path

notion of God that makes us something more than a collection of particles.

Where my opinion may differ from others is that I believe we have one life - one shot at it all. If we experience any additional lives, the slate is clean. I think occasionally we meet very wise people on the path that can help us see and understand ways of more frequently traveling the path and or living a very simple and happy life. Interestingly enough, we sometimes meet people from the past and perhaps even the future on our path. That's because the path exists outside of time and people's thoughts and legacies transcend the physical limits of life.

I know this sounds crazy, so let me explain at least the aspect of the past. Imagine you wander into your attic to rummage among your great-grandparent's things. Even if you never met them, you might get a sense of their life and experiences. They may have a legacy and you might find them, symbolically speaking, standing right there on your path with you.

Where the ego comes into play, when we recognize it, is that our self wants and tries to improve upon the wonderful walk on the path and ultimately leads to a deviation from it. This is a cycle. We are ill fated to repeat it over and over again, unless we reprogram ourselves to resist the ego.

I'll risk being very abstract here. Our futures unfold from the past. If we develop awareness, we can see the future in the past and present before it becomes the actual future. There are signs all around us. Ideas develop over time. If you think back to the concept of tribal theory I spoke about earlier, you can currently see people floating theories out to smaller groups. If these theories start gaining acceptance then they spread to the masses. They will become the future. We sometimes meet these people on our path, and they are the originators of what is to come.

To spend time on the path, we must let go more and more. We must deny complexity and keep modern life from consuming us. I was listening to my youngest step-daughter the other day, and she was distressed because there was too much good TV to watch and she just didn't know how she was going to be able to consume it all, despite having recorded on the Digital Video Recorder.

And that's just the problem, when do we just say no to all the superficial distractions and let go? It's a bit like a drug if you think about it; it attempts to pacify us. If a mastermind criminal wanted to enslave the world with a socioeconomic system, they could hardly have designed a better trap than the one we live in today. A large portion of the business world needs for us to believe materialism is the answer to all our problems. If not, the economy will go belly up.

We enslave ourselves to materials and the way of life that is advertised and promoted to us. We view this as the reward for our efforts. I won't say reward for hard work because many people despise the idea of hard work and find easier ways to obtain the advertised promise. For those working hard, the trap is even more difficult to escape. All that hard work, it just creates more want for escape and for the worldly material things and dreams we are constantly sold and programmed to crave. We are taught to believe these things will fulfill all of our needs and solve all of our problems. What if we are the problem and our thinking is what creates all the needs we are attempting to satisfy?

The Path

Because of the economic implications, we can't deal with a mass mindset change since it would cause life and society as we know it to crumble! At stake is Maslow's hierarchy of human needs as we are tightly tied to today's socioeconomic structure. Maslow didn't intend it to be this way. What we consider basic and essential today is far different from how it was defined decades ago. Visit a poverty stricken nation and you'll soon discover people happy and smiling for the simplest amenities that we take for granted!

Following the path requires what many would refer to as blind faith and commitment. This can be very uncomfortable. This book helps ready you for a life on the path which amounts to a mixture of washing away the artificial programming, simplifying your life, learning to say no more to the modern day rat race, embracing the wisdom to make sound decisions and finding the faith to follow your heart and path.

Maybe it will be easier to suggest to you that the path is your heart and soul and this concept resides apart from religion and beliefs about God. It's true though, like myself, if your hearts is tied to God then we come full circle. Perhaps in the grand design we must look to our hearts and inner soul and our God will instill the purity in our hearts and souls to find and walk our own path.

I've made this my last major chapter by design. Many of you may scratch your heads on this chapter and wonder why it's so different from all others. The book itself is about taking control of your emotions and feelings. This chapter suggests that you let go and not worry so much about control. It's ambiguous and my hope for you is that you stew on all of this STUFF I've thrown at you. Maybe a different way to state this is that the rest of the book teaches you how to deal with all of your issues in life and prepares you to embrace your path by enabling you to let go.

The best analogy I can provide to you on this is to think about the process of cleaning a room. It may be complicated to get it all cleaned up, organized and simplified. Once you do, then there is less you need to worry about! You can move about freely and if you have planned carefully and done the work, it should be easier to maintain order as you move forward.

Swing at that funky curve ball; accept that you'll miss it many times before you actually hit it. Take some walks, find some solitude and think things through.

Dare to make changes in your life, simplify, enjoy the simple pleasures life can afford us when we aren't blinded by the machine. Learn to see and become aware of the path when you are on it. It's a bit of a contradiction to become aware on the path because in many ways the path is about the abandonment of awareness. I've learned to recognize the path shortly after stepping off of it. I then think about what brought me to walk its comforting trail for a bit. See and follow your path as much as you can.

Understand that you can't always be on the path. Perhaps the goal is to get as much time on it as possible and never let the societal super structure drag you too far away!

Follow your heart and use your mind and common sense as well, they will duel with each other and it is the path itself that guides us through the grayness of it all!

Life Meanings

Life Meanings is the condensed genesis for this book. It's more a less a diatribe that I created almost 10 years ago and use as a container to note and condense the lessons I learn in life.

Life Meanings

It is both sad and funny at the same time how we often spend our lives dreaming about the future while the present passes us by.

We never seem to find the time to enjoy what we have for we seem more focused on what we can obtain. We feel certain that these things will make a difference but more often they simply mark another milestone and fall to insignificance.

It's odd in life how people value the importance of some people more than others among the billions of us and how seldom two people find each other important. I think sometimes it's why we all have so few friends. We seldom tell people how we feel about them. We get so fearful of sharing feelings and of the communication process itself, being hesitant to share ideas and feeling worried how we'll be perceived. I believe you will find that people value you more when you value them more.

Many times we feel that others are responsible for the troubles in our lives and quickly seek to lay blame on them. It is my belief that this is one of the lower points we can find ourselves in because it relates to so many other of the issues with regard to control, expectations, respect and ones focus in life.

Often we build expectations in our minds for people that exceed their true nature and capabilities and we blame them for failing to live up to them. This is a certain source of unhappiness we create ourselves and yet hold others responsible for.

Trust is greatly linked to expectations. If your expectations are unrealistic, you are likely to feel like your trust has been betrayed when someone fails to meet expectations. Trust, like respect, is earned and one must believe and trust in others before others will believe and trust in them. Trust though, is a risk and if one has no trust then they will find themselves surrounded by walls, isolated and imprisoned.

Betrayal is the beast of all emotions; no other mountain is harder to pass than the feelings that come with it. It provides fuel for anger, sorrow, disappointment and regret, loss and even rage. It can leave us wandering aimlessly asking why. In these darkest moments, one must center themselves, confront the betrayer, reflect upon themselves how it was they were betrayed and whether they actually betrayed themselves and then let go and forgive. The single greatest obstacle is truly being able to forgive the betrayer, and I believe you absolutely must do this, for until you do, you will carry the betrayers' burden for them. I believe you must let fate and karma reconcile betrayal.

Sometimes we can feel lonely even when we are surrounded by friends and family and the reason for it eludes us. Some say it's because we lack spirituality and fail by not subscribing to a higher purpose. We look to some greater force than ourselves for condolences and subscribe ourselves to one holistic solution. However, often we become lonely again after we lose our resolve or the subscription becomes mundane.

Sometimes we feel we do not get the respect we deserve. We value respect and often demand it even when we have not earned it. We often wish to be treated better than how we treat others. I believe there is a simple formula which governs respect; simply stated, it follows that you probably only deserve 1/4 the respect you think you should have and one gets about 1/4 as much respect as one gives.

There are times when we feel we cannot make the tough decisions, directionless, without will and lost in the forest of life. At these moments I remind myself that not all the decisions have to be made immediately. Plotting out small steps helps one grope their way far enough along in the dark to find a source of light.

Change and its ability to consume us are inevitable. Change is the paint brush of time and our lives are the canvas which its strokes are cast upon. By looking for what lies beyond the change, preparing for it through planning and by finding what will be a positive afterwards, change shall pass more swiftly.

Love and devotion are like the pendulum on the clock of time, swaying back and forth in its motion but always moving time forward. We make friends, we have best friends, we take lovers, we sometimes transcend beyond love to a higher form of friendship full of both love and devotion. Love is possessive by its nature and often can be blissful as well as breed selfishness and jealousy.

I believe the higher forms of love are unselfish, and place those we love before ourselves, even at cost to ourselves or the loss of love. That said though, love is essential to the human spirit as it brings stability to our lives, and it is why we seek to hold on to it for as long as we can as there is no other feeling quite like it. To reject love is to kill one's spirit. We must also have and respect love of ourselves as it is essential to the human spirit as well. We must love and be at peace with ourselves before we can love others.

We are granted this passage of life with a limited number of years to live and explore. When we are aware of these great questions and their consequences and their ability to absorb us, we often stand helpless in their wake.

Meaning is our beliefs and therefore, our lives.

We are self-centered which, I have learned, in part is the reason these truths are inevitable. In the end, we are captivated by them because it is us and us alone who they occupy and master. Through the exploration of others and our inner fears, we can broaden our horizons.

Life Meanings

We must remember that the more we seek to control the more helpless we will feel. We can build a fortress around us and attempt to control the influences and emotions that are allowed to enter but the self-awareness of doing so becomes a source of pain in itself, and we miss out on the grander scope of life.

Sometimes when we let go of it all, life can become simple and beautiful. It is inevitable that this will be short lived though, for it is the valleys and change that make the peaks so great. I think that often we simply live on level ground and life's clock ticks away on us. I believe that's okay and that not every moment has to be charged with intensity and is at the core of the reason why quiet and solitude can be so refreshing.

There are times when we become consumed by life's trials and pains. The realization that wounds can be healed and that time itself is a large part of the cure can make the healing process easier. With time all things pass and the realization that this is true is very powerful. By asking ourselves about the sorrow we are drowning in and what lies beyond the pain we can be well again sooner.

Perhaps the greatest source of disharmony in our lives comes from us. We often look for external explanations to account for this disruption such as bad luck, karma or other reasons. Sometimes we must look within ourselves and ask what we are doing for ourselves to create harmony. We should ask what people and influences we are accepting into our lives and what actions we are taking, regardless of any misfortunate or circumstances we believe block our path.

We must realize that regardless of how we arrived, we will not be happy until we depart again. To escape disharmony is no easy feat, short of luck that is rare, it takes concentrated effort above and beyond that we normally expend to move beyond its barriers. If we wish to move ahead, we must enable ourselves to do so through planning and action.

Perhaps the greatest realization one can have is that true happiness is simplistic, distilled from life and emotion itself and just raw and pure. When we let go of the material things that we compulsively drive for and constantly seek and accept the very simple beauty life offers us then we can feel free, happy and one with ourselves and others and all that surrounds us.

There are times such as these when we seek the meaning of life even though we believe sometimes it's a fruitless journey. It is us ourselves, our true heart and spirit, our beliefs that give meaning and purpose to our existence. This is a circle that we find ourselves traversing throughout our life journey.

Often we run around in circles in our mind thinking and thinking of how to resolve the great debates that shape our lives. Sometimes we feel as if we are programmed by society, parents and even our genetics. We can spend years trying to override such programming. Perhaps the heart is the key to true enlightenment. When we follow our heart more often, then the spirit can lead the mind, and that it often leads us to peace and balance.

Mostly there are questions without answers, and perhaps it is this mystery that is the very essence of life itself, a quest we embark upon, seeking elusive answers and surprises at every turn, the sum of which is what makes life the greatest journey of them all.

Life Meanings

Consciousness is what we do, feel and experience when we are not thinking. Spirit springs from within, from our hearts, generating feelings and balancing our logic.

We are limited by the sum of our experiences and the mindset they create. They blind us from new dimensions with the veil of fog they leave us to look through.

We must not limit ourselves or others by living in a world of black and white, or simply right and wrong. We will only travel beyond today's thinking by daring to think ahead of these limiting concepts and through the development of different and changing mindsets.

If these words are true then we must continue to calmly seek and explore, yet, also ensure we savor every moment we have whether it be good or bad. Be true to your heart and inner spirit and to those you love and whom you care for. Feel life, don't simply think it away! Live a little more for now and ponder what might be a little less. Don't let life pass you by.

Life is sweet, grand, painful, mysterious, complicated and only bound by the limits we believe in! What more meaning do we really need?

Nymph Lake
Mark Abraham
Rocky Mountain National Park, Colorado 2005

Sitting by a mountain lake with my thoughts, experiencing a scene we might normally find only in dreams. A chipmunk crawls up on me begging for a bite of my lunch in an offer of momentary friendship.

Perfect Imperfection

Nothing is more perfect than imperfection!

I hope you haven't grown tired of my little sayings. I find that some people feel exhausted by them. They'll look at me with a tilted head and a what in the world are you talking expression when I lay these self-proclaimed gems on them!

As with all of them, I'll try to be brief!

Man's quest and obsession with perfection is long and storied. This quest for perfection is sometimes endless and often fruitless. In many cases the device that works 100% of the time holds little more value than the one which works 99.9% of the time.

A Mind for Life

Perhaps you've heard of the 80/20 rule. It basically states that achieving 80% of the goal is most crucial to success - the last 20% can be addressed over time.

It's futile to build a perfect mousetrap because as soon as you do, a new kind of rat that can't get snared in your "perfect" trap will come along. As trite as that may sound, it's not really the little gem I want you to consider now.

Maybe you've stopped and looked at the pattern on a leaf and considered it to be flawed because a caterpillar chomped a bite out of it or one finger of the leaf was longer than the other. Maybe you were walking and saw a lopsided tree and you thought about how much nicer it would look if it were evenly balanced and formed.

Take a deep breath and imagine a world where everything is perfect: all the leaves are formed evenly and bite free, all the trees are straight and everything is perfectly symmetrical. Wouldn't this perfection become boring? In this world, what would our notion of perfection be? Would we begin to crave variation instead of perfection?

If you can grab that thought, then you might just get my little gem. You see, imperfection is really perfection. It proves to me that there is substance to the design of all we see and experience in life.

Imperfection is the spice of life; it's what makes everything different and enables the notion of poetic beauty. How much more perfect could you really get?

Perfect Imperfection

I dare you to see life differently! Embrace its flaws; embrace the downs with the ups and the lows with the highs. Take note of the road that is flat and realize how interesting it still is. Appreciate the norm so that you can appreciate the exceptions.

Develop A Mind For Life!

About The Author

By day I manage information systems development and technology. I truly enjoy breaking apart problems and developing solutions for customers in my work. I also thrive off of interacting with others both in my work and in my personal life.

A Mind for Life

These days I enjoy time with my family, just living and experiencing life. I feel fortunate to have found the woman of my dreams and for all the wonderment and love of the four girls she brought with her into my life.

I once dabbled as a part-time photographer, graphic designer and website designer. I have provided all the photography and graphics in this book. As a former member of the Professional Photographers of America, I obtained a few awards for images I submitted in international print competitions. You can see some of my other work in the film Last Breath (2010) where I shot some of the stills and the photography for the family pictures in the house.

I once fell head over heels for astronomy and discovered and named a few asteroids. During those nights, I also helped professional astronomers around the world by building a remote controlled observatory in my backyard, where I discovered asteroids and completed follow up work for the Harvard Minor Planet Center.

A Mind For Life is my first book and, true to my nature, I established a website where you can visit, find other works and information about me and join in the discussion.

Placing all the fun and cool things in my life aside, writing this book has been the best achievement of my life. While some of the things I've mentioned may sound like significant accomplishments, the most important thing about them is how they shaped and changed the way I see life.

About The Author

In my humble opinion, the accolades themselves don't offer much in the bigger picture. It's my hope that this is what you take away most about me, the author!

Sunset Tree
Mark Abraham
Paola, Kansas 2006

The branches extend into the backdrop of the sunset and another day fades away. Work done, results checked off and the crickets singing their song of sleep. An honest day ends in peace! You feel alive, humble, and serene! All are working together in peaceful harmony throughout your mind and spirit! You have developed A Mind For Life!

Thanks for reading my book!

Please visit my website www.AMindForLife.com or www.am4l.com

www.ingramcontent.com/pod-product-compliance
Lightning Source LLC
LaVergne TN
LVHW051541070426
835507LV00021B/2356